Skills Worksheet

Directed Reading

Section: The Reptilian Body

Complete each statement by underlining the correct term or phrase in the brackets.

1. Reptiles have a strong, bony skeleton and toes [with / without] claws.

2. Reptiles are [endothermic / ectothermic].

3. The skin of reptiles is [watertight / moist].

4. The eggs of reptiles are most similar to the eggs of [birds / amphibians].

5. Reptiles respire through [gills / lungs].

6. In the hearts of most reptiles, the ventricle is [completely / partly] divided by a septum.

7. Reptiles reproduce by [internal / external] fertilization.

Read each question, and write your answer in the space provided.

8. How do reptiles respond to very cold weather?

____

____

____

9. Why must reptiles absorb heat from their surroundings?

____

____

____

10. Why are reptiles better able to move on land than are amphibians?

____

____

____

| Directed Reading *continued*

In the space provided, write the letter of the description that best matches the term or phrase.

______ **11.** amnion

______ **12.** yolk sac

______ **13.** allantois

______ **14.** chorion

a. allows oxygen to enter the egg and carbon dioxide to leave the egg

b. encloses the embryo within a watery environment

c. contains the developing embryo's food supply

d. stores waste products from the embryo and serves as the embryo's organ for gas exchange

In the space provided, explain how the terms in each pair differ in meaning.

15. oviparous, ovoviviparous

____

____

____

____

16. internal fertilization, external fertilization

____

____

____

____

Directed Reading

Section: Today's Reptiles

Read each question, and write your answer in the space provided.

1. What is the distinguishing characteristic of snakes and lizards?

____

____

____

2. Why is it likely that snakes evolved from lizards?

____

____

____

3. How do snakes kill their prey?

____

____

____

4. What are the four families of venomous snakes?

____

____

____

5. What is a pit organ, and how does it help the timber rattlesnake catch prey?

____

____

____

6. What are Jacobson's organs, and how do they help the timber rattlesnake catch prey?

____

____

7. Why is it advantageous for crocodiles and alligators to have eyes high on the sides of the head and nostrils on top of the snout?

____

____

____

____

8. How do crocodilians differ from other reptiles in the way they care for their young?

____

____

9. What is a tuatara?

____

____

____

In the space provided, explain how the terms in each pair differ in meaning.

10. turtle, tortoise

____

____

11. carapace, plastron

____

____

Directed Reading

Section: Characteristics and Diversity of Birds

Complete each statement by underlining the correct term or phrase in the brackets.

1. The wings of birds are modified from [forelimbs / ribs and breastbones].

2. The feet and legs of birds are covered with [feathers / scales].

3. The skeletons of birds are [lightweight / made of cartilage].

4. The metabolism of birds is [ectothermic / endothermic].

5. Birds have [inefficient / highly efficient] lungs.

6. The ventricles of birds are [completely / partially] divided by a septum.

Read each question, and write your answer in the space provided.

7. Distinguish between contour feathers and down feathers.

____

____

____

____

8. Why do birds pull their feathers through their beaks in a process called preening?

____

____

____

9. Why are birds so light compared with similarly sized mammals?

____

10. Why do birds have a higher body temperature than do mammals?

____

____

____

| Directed Reading *continued*

11. What features of a bird's respiratory system make it highly efficient?

____

____

____

12. How do birds benefit from having a septum in their ventricles?

____

____

____

Write the correct bird type from the list below in the space next to its characteristics.

birds of prey   long-legged waders   songbirds

ducks   parrots   woodpeckers

hummingbirds

_________________________ **13.** short, thick, strong beak for seed cracking

_________________________ **14.** legs so small it cannot walk; tiny feet

_________________________ **15.** a strong, chisel-like beak

_________________________ **16.** strong toes, two pointing forward and two pointing backward, adapted for perching, climbing, and holding food

_________________________ **17.** powerful talons and a curved, pointed beak

_________________________ **18.** a long, flattened, rounded bill; three toes linked by webs

_________________________ **19.** long legs; toes spread out over a large area to support bird on soft surfaces

Active Reading

Section: The Reptilian Body

Read the passage below. Then answer the questions that follow.

Reptiles' ectothermic metabolism is too slow to generate enough heat to warm their body, so reptiles must absorb heat from their surroundings. As a result, a reptile's body temperature is largely determined by the temperature of its environment. Many reptiles regulate their temperature behaviorally, by basking in the sun to warm up or seeking shade to cool down. A lizard can maintain a relatively constant body temperature throughout the day by moving between sunlight and shade. At very low temperatures, most reptiles become sluggish and unable to function. Intolerance of cold generally limits their geographical range and, in temperate climates, forces them to remain inactive through the winter.

SKILL: RECOGNIZING CAUSE AND EFFECT

Two independent events can be linked through a cause-and-effect relationship. The first event to occur, or cause, triggers a second event, or effect, to happen. Identify the effect of each cause-and-effect relationship described below.

1. Cause: A reptile's ectothermic metabolism is too slow to generate enough heat to warm its body.

Effect: ____

____

2. Cause: A reptile basks in the sun.

Effect: ____

____

3. Cause: A lizard spends part of its day in sunlight and part in shade.

Effect: ____

____

In the space provided, write the letter of the term or phrase that best completes the statement.

________ **4.** Most reptiles deal with the cold winters of temperate climates by
    a. remaining inactive.   **c.** changing their metabolism.
    b. migrating.   **d.** Both (a) and (b)

Active Reading

Section: Today's Reptiles

Read the passage below. Then answer the questions that follow.

Turtles and tortoises differ from other reptiles in that their bodies are encased within a hard, bony, protective shell. Many of them can pull their head and legs into the shell for effective protection from predators. While most tortoises have a dome-shaped shell, water-dwelling turtles have a streamlined, disk-shaped shell that permits rapid maneuvering in water. Turtles and tortoises lack teeth but have jaws covered by sharp plates. Many are herbivores, but some, such as the snapping turtle, are aggressive carnivores.

Today's turtles and tortoises differ little from the earliest known turtle fossils, which are more than 200 million years old. This evolutionary stability may reflect the adaptive aspects of the basic shell-covered body structure of turtles and tortoises.

SKILL: READING EFFECTIVELY

Read each question, and write your answer in the space provided.

1. How are turtles and tortoises different from other reptiles?

____

____

____

2. Are all turtle shells and tortoise shells alike? Give examples.

____

____

____

In the space provided, write the letter of the term or phrase that best completes the statement.

_______ **3.** Snapping turtles, unlike some other turtles and tortoises

    a. are herbivores.

    b. have a unique shell design.

    c. are water-dwellers.

    d. are carnivores.

Active Reading

Section: Characteristics and Diversity of Birds

Read the passage below. Then answer the questions that follow.

When birds fly, they use a considerable amount of energy. Since birds often fly for long periods of time, their cellular demand for energy exceeds that of even the most active mammal.

Reptiles meet their increased need for oxygen with lungs that have a larger surface area than the lungs of amphibians. But there is a limit to how much the efficiency of a lung can be improved just by increasing its surface area. Another way to increase the efficiency of a lung is to have air pass over its respiratory surface in one direction only, just as water flows over a fish's gills in one direction. This is what happens in birds. One-way air flow is possible in birds because they have air sacs connected to their lungs.

There are two important advantages to one-way air flow. First, the lungs are exposed only to air that is almost fully oxygenated, increasing the amount of oxygen transported to the body cells. Second, the flow of blood in the lungs runs in a different direction than the flow of air. While the flow of air and blood are not completely opposite, the difference in direction does increase oxygen absorption.

SKILL: READING EFFECTIVELY

Read the question and write your answer in the space provided.

1. What are the advantages of one-way air flow?

____

____

____

____

In the space provided, write the letter of the term or phrase that best completes the statement.

_______ **2.** In a bird's lungs, air and blood flow in
  a. completely opposite directions.
  b. the same direction.
  c. different directions.
  d. parallel paths.

Vocabulary Review

In the space provided, write the letter of the description that best matches the term or phrase.

_______ **1.** amniotic egg

_______ **2.** oviparous

_______ **3.** ovoviviparous

_______ **4.** carapace

_______ **5.** plastron

a. top part of the shell of a turtle

b. encloses the embryo in a watery environment

c. bottom part of the shell of a turtle

d. meaning the female retains eggs within her body until shortly before or after hatching

e. meaning the young hatch from eggs

Complete each statement by writing the correct term or phrase in the space provided.

6. The body of a young bird is covered by _____________________ feathers.

7. The body of an adult bird gets its shape from _____________________ feathers.

8. A bird protects and waterproofs its feathers by pulling them through its beak and covering them with oil from its _____________________

_____________________ .

Science Skills

Analyzing Information/Interpreting Tables

The table below lists some of the characteristics of the four living orders of reptiles and of birds. Use the table to answer questions 1–6.

Characteristic	Crocodilians	Lizards and snakes	Tuataras	Turtles and tortoises	Birds
Amniotic egg?	yes	yes	yes	yes	yes
Care for young?	yes	no	no	no	yes
Cloaca?	yes	yes	yes	yes	yes
Feathers?	no	no	no	no	yes
Fertilization	internal	internal	internal	internal	internal
Heart ventricle	completely divided	partly divided	partly divided	partly divided	completely divided
Metabolism	ectothermic	ectothermic	ectothermic	ectothermic	endothermic
Number of legs	four	four or none	four	four	two
Scales?	yes	yes	yes	yes	yes (on legs and feet)
Teeth?	yes	yes	yes	no	no
Wings?	no	no	no	no	yes

Read each question, and write your answer in the space provided.

1. Which characteristics are shared by all reptiles and birds?

____

____

2. Which characteristics are found in all reptiles but not in birds?

____

____

3. Which characteristics are found in birds but not in reptiles?

____

____

| Science Skills *continued*

---

4. Some biologists have proposed that birds and reptiles should be grouped in the same class of vertebrates. What information in the table supports that proposal?

____

____

____

____

5. Other biologists argue that reptiles and birds belong in different classes. What information in the table supports that argument?

____

____

____

____

6. A third group of biologists has suggested that birds and one of the reptilian orders belong in the same class, and that the other three reptilian orders belong in a different class. If this classification scheme was accepted, which reptilian order do you think should be put in the same class as birds? Use the information in the table to support your decision.

____

____

____

____

Concept Mapping

Using the terms and phrases provided below, complete the concept map showing the characteristics of reptiles and birds.

ectothermic	hollow bones	metabolism	skeleton
feathers	internal folds	one-way air flow	solid bones
hard shell	leathery shell	scales	

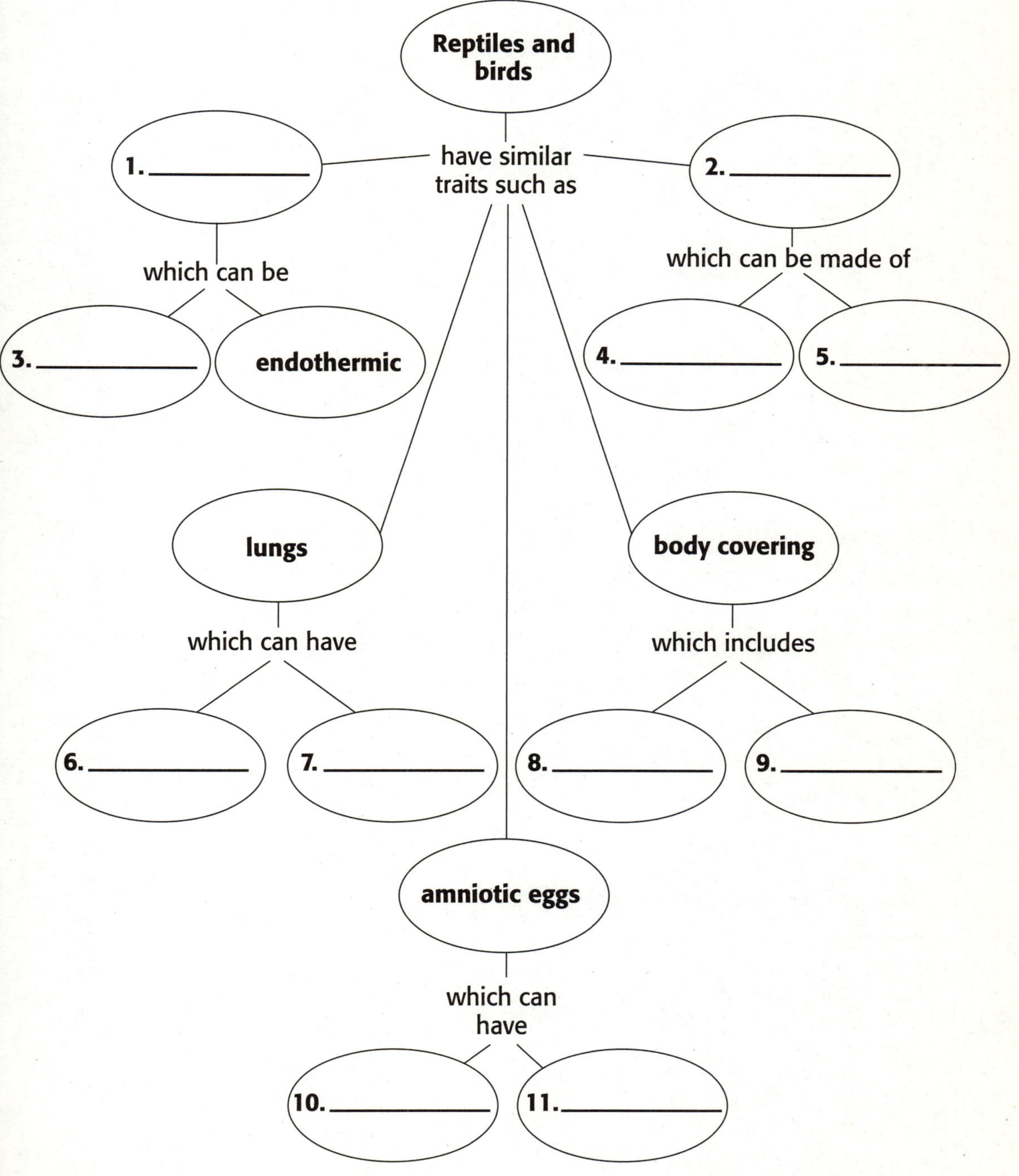

Critical Thinking

Work-Alikes

In the space provided, write the letter of the term or phrase that best describes how each numbered item functions.

_______ **1.** moving between sun and shade

_______ **2.** crocodile eyes

_______ **3.** bird breastbone

_______ **4.** completely divided heart ventricles of crocodiles and birds

a. keel of a boat

b. double-basin kitchen sink

c. thermostat

d. periscope on a submarine

Cause and Effect

In the space provided, write the letter of the term or phrase that best matches each cause or effect given below.

Cause	Effect
5. _______________	limited geographical range and inactivity during winter
6. _______________	amniotic egg
7. evolution of lizards	_______________
8. streamlined, disk-shaped shell	_______________
9. _______________	increased oxygen absorption
10. _______________	ability to run swiftly after prey

a. rapid turning in water

b. legs positioned directly under body

c. need for moist environment during development

d. snakes

e. one-way air flow in bird lungs

f. reptiles' intolerance of cold weather

Trade-offs

In the space provided, write the letter of the bad news item that best matches each numbered good news item below.

Good News

_______ **11.** Reptiles live successfully in warm regions.

_______ **12.** Reptiles have evolved watertight skin.

_______ **13.** Heat from the environment incubates eggs.

Bad News

a. Terrestrial animals face problem of water loss through skin.

b. They cannot live in the coldest regions of the world.

c. Most reptile eggs receive no protection by parents.

Linkages

In the spaces provided, write the letters of the two terms or phrases that are linked together by the term or phrase in the middle. The choices can be placed in any order.

14. _______ ovoviviparous _______

15. _______ turtle _______

16. _______ alligator _______

17. _______ re-linking barbules _______

18. _______ higher metabolism _______

19. _______ crocodilian heart with complete

   division of ventricles _______

a. reptilian heart with incomplete division of ventricle

b. deposits oil on feathers

c. carapace

d. preening behavior in birds

e. crocodile

f. give birth to live young

g. bird heart with complete division of ventricle

h. caiman

i. increased energy requirements for flight permitted

j. plastron

k. birds maintain high body temperatures

l. nourishment from yolk sac

Analogies

An analogy is a relationship between two pairs of terms or phrases written as a : b :: c : d. The symbol : is read as "is to," and the symbol :: is read as "as." In the space provided, write the letter of the pair of terms or phrases that best completes the analogy shown.

_______**20.** amniotic egg : reptiles and birds ::
   a. movable eyelids : snakes   **c.** scales : mammals
   b. legs : snakes   **d.** feathers : birds

_______**21.** constrictor snakes : suffocation ::
   a. king snakes : venom   **c.** boas : venom
   b. rattlesnakes : venom   **d.** copperheads : suffocation

_______**22.** carnivorous birds : sharp beaks
   a. ducks : curved talons   **c.** finches : long, slender beaks
   b. ducks : chisel-like beaks   **d.** finches : short, thick beaks

Test Prep Pretest

In the space provided, write the letter of the term or phrase that best completes each statement or best answers each question.

______ **1.** Tuataras are members of the reptile order
- **a.** Chelonia.
- **b.** Squamata.
- **c.** Rhynchocephalia.
- **d.** Crocodilia.

______ **2.** In the raising of their young, crocodiles most closely resemble
- **a.** turtles.
- **b.** lizards.
- **c.** snakes.
- **d.** birds.

______ **3.** All reptiles EXCEPT crocodilians have
- **a.** a partially divided ventricle.
- **b.** lungs.
- **c.** overlapping scales.
- **d.** watertight skin.

______ **4.** Which of the following is NOT true of a turtle's shell?
- **a.** Vertebrae are fused to the inside of the carapace.
- **b.** The shell provides support for muscle attachment.
- **c.** The carapace is always dome shaped.
- **d.** The shell is made of fused plates of bone.

______ **5.** The second chamber in the stomach of a bald eagle is known as the
- **a.** crop.
- **b.** gizzard.
- **c.** esophagus.
- **d.** cloaca.

In the space provided, write the letter of the description that best matches the term or phrase.

______ **6.** contour feathers

______ **7.** plastron

______ **8.** Jacobson's organs

______ **9.** carapace

- **a.** detect odor of chemicals to help snakes follow prey
- **b.** give an adult bird its shape
- **c.** the bottom part of a turtle or tortoise shell
- **d.** the top part of a turtle or tortoise shell

| Test Prep Pretest *continued*

Complete each statement by writing the correct term or phrase in the space provided.

10. Because the _______________________ in a bird's heart is completely divided, oxygen-rich and oxygen-poor blood are kept completely _______________________ .

11. A timber rattlesnake's venom contains _______________________ , which destroy red blood cells and cause internal hemorrhaging.

12. A long, flattened, rounded bill, as found in _______________________ , is adapted for sieving.

13. Feathers are modified reptilian _______________________ .

14. Most reptiles cannot live in avery cold regions because they are

_______________________ .

15. Reptiles, birds, and three species of mammals reproduce by means of

_______________________ eggs, which is evidence that they share a

common _______________________ .

16. Many reptiles are _______________________ , meaning their young hatch from eggs.

17. Some species of snakes and lizards are _______________________ , which means the female retains the eggs within her body until shortly before hatching, or the eggs may hatch within the female's body.

Read each question, and write your answer in the space provided.

18. List the four orders of present-day reptiles, and give an example of each.

____

____

____

____

____

Test Prep Pretest *continued*

19. Describe the structure and function of a turtle's shell.

____

____

____

____

____

____

20. Which is more efficient—a bird lung or a reptile lung? Explain.

____

____

____

____

____

____

Quiz

Section: The Reptilian Body

In the space provided, write the letter of the description that best matches the term or phrase.

_______ **1.** amniotic egg

_______ **2.** allantois

_______ **3.** amnion

_______ **4.** chorion

_______ **5.** yolk sac

_______ **6.** oviparous

a. sac that stores an embryo's waste products

b. structure that supplies nourishment to an embryo

c. reproductive structure containing water and food for a developing embryo

d. membrane that allows gases to enter and leave an egg

e. describing reptiles whose young hatch from eggs

f. enclosure that cushions an embryo in a watery environment

In the space provided, write the letter of the term or phrase that best completes each statement or best answers each question.

_______ **7.** The problem of sperm and eggs drying out on land is solved in reptiles by which of the following?
  a. internal fertilization
  b. the amniotic egg
  c. overlapping scales
  d. Both (a) and (b)

_______ **8.** Compared with the legs of amphibians, the legs of reptiles are positioned
  a. closer to the head.
  b. farther from the head.
  c. farther apart.
  d. more directly under the body.

_______ **9.** Lizards decrease their body temperature by
  a. absorbing heat from their environment.
  b. increasing their rate of metabolism.
  c. staying in the shade.
  d. basking in the sun.

_______ **10.** The skin of reptiles
  a. consists of light, flexible scales.
  b. loses a lot of water through evaporation.
  c. functions as a respiratory surface.
  d. All of the above

Quiz

Section: Today's Reptiles

In the space provided, write the letter of the description that best matches the term or phrase.

_______ **1.** fang

_______ **2.** caiman

_______ **3.** tuatara

_______ **4.** tortoise

_______ **5.** Jacobson's organ

_______ **6.** anaconda

a. reptile in the order Crocodilia

b. reptile in the order Squamata

c. chemical-sensing depression in a rattlesnake's mouth

d. hollow tooth used to inject venom

e. lizardlike reptile native to New Zealand

f. toothless reptile with dome-shaped shell

In the space provided, write the letter of the term or phrase that best completes each statement or best answers each question.

_______ **7.** During the Cretaceous period, snakes probably evolved from
    a. turtles.
    b. lizards.
    c. dinosaurs.
    d. alligators.

_______ **8.** Which structure does a timber rattlesnake use to locate warm-bodied animals in total darkness?
    a. venom gland
    b. tongue
    c. pit organ
    d. rattle

_______ **9.** Which of the following characteristics distinguishes crocodilians from other reptiles?
    a. Crocodilians care for their young after hatching.
    b. Crocodilians are ectothermic.
    c. Crocodilians have dry, watertight skin.
    d. Crocodilians have amniotic eggs.

_______ **10.** Unlike most reptiles, members of the order Rhynchocephalia are
    a. scaleless.
    b. aquatic.
    c. most active at low temperatures.
    d. endothermic.

Quiz

Section: Characteristics and Diversity of Birds

In the space provided, write the letter of the description that best matches the term or phrase.

_______ **1.** hummingbird

_______ **2.** bird of prey

_______ **3.** woodpecker

_______ **4.** long-legged wader

_______ **5.** songbird

_______ **6.** parrot

a. thin, slightly curved beak

b. long, slender, spear-shaped beak

c. short, stout, hooked beak

d. strong, chisel-like beak

e. toes that can cling to branches; one toe points backward

f. powerful, curved talons

In the space provided, write the letter of the term or phrase that best completes each statement or best answers each question.

_______ **7.** Birds satisfy their increased need for oxygen by having
    a. air sacs.
    b. one-way air flow through the lungs.
    c. a completely divided ventricle.
    d. All of the above

_______ **8.** The excretory system of birds
    a. is lightweight but inefficient.
    b. stores liquid wastes in a bladder.
    c. converts nitrogenous wastes to uric acid.
    d. absorbs nitrogenous wastes from the cloaca.

_______ **9.** Down feathers are used mostly for
    a. providing lift for flight.
    b. conserving body heat.
    c. attracting mates.
    d. All of the above

_______ **10.** Which of the following is NOT an adaptation of birds for flight?
    a. webbed feet
    b. keeled breastbone
    c. thin, hollow bones
    d. fused collarbones

Chapter Test

Reptiles and Birds

In the space provided, write the letter of the description that best matches the term or phrase.

_______ **1.** pit organs

_______ **2.** Jacobson's organs

_______ **3.** ovoviviparous

_______ **4.** oviparous

_______ **5.** air sacs

_______ **6.** Chelonia

_______ **7.** preen gland

a. retaining fertilized eggs within the female's body until the eggs hatch

b. structures on a rattlesnake that can detect the odor of chemicals

c. structure that secretes oil to be spread over a bird's feathers

d. structures that permit one-way flow of air through a bird's lungs

e. order of reptiles that includes turtles and tortoises

f. structures on a rattlesnake that can detect infrared radiation

g. producing offspring that hatch from eggs outside the female's body

In the space provided, write the letter of the term or phrase that best completes each statement or best answers each question.

_______ **8.** Which of the following is NOT a method that reptiles use to regulate their body temperature?
   a. basking in the sunshine to warm themselves
   b. resting in the shade to cool themselves
   c. generating large amounts of heat through metabolism
   d. absorbing heat from their surroundings

_______ **9.** Crocodilians are distinguished from other reptiles by having
   a. air sacs.
   b. a fully divided ventricle.
   c. a partially divided ventricle.
   d. shelled eggs.

_______ **10.** Which of the following is true of snakes?
   a. They have limbs.
   b. They have movable eyelids.
   c. They lack external ears.
   d. All of the above

| Chapter Test *continued*

_______**11.** Birds have which of the following?
    a. feathers
    b. fused collarbones
    c. a keeled breastbone
    d. All of the above

_______**12.** A bird's skeleton is
    a. composed of thin, hollow bones.
    b. more rigid than a reptile's skeleton.
    c. composed of many fused bones.
    d. All of the above

_______**13.** A bird's crop
    a. temporarily stores food.
    b. is the first chamber of its stomach.
    c. is critical for flight.
    d. excretes uric acid.

_______**14.** In flying birds, large flight muscles are directly attached to
    a. leg muscles.
    b. feathers.
    c. the keeled breastbone.
    d. air sacs.

_______**15.** Unlike other reptiles, crocodilians
    a. care for their young after the young hatch.
    b. use internal fertilization.
    c. are oviparous.
    d. are ectothermic.

_______**16.** One adaptation that helps reptiles succeed on land is
    a. gills.
    b. watertight skin.
    c. external fertilization.
    d. endothermic metabolism.

_______**17.** What characteristics are required for a beak that is used to tear apart
prey or vegetation?
    a. long, spear-shaped
    b. hooked, curved, and pointed
    c. chisel-shaped
    d. thin, slightly curved

Chapter Test *continued*

Questions 18–20 refer to the figure below, which shows the structure of a bird.

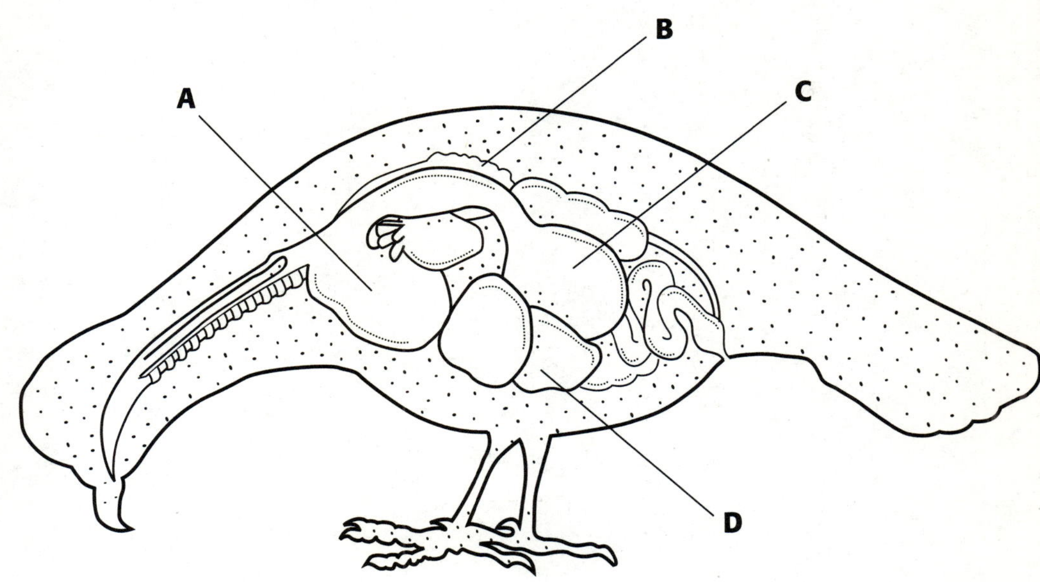

_______**18.** The structure labeled *A* is the
    a. gizzard.
    b. liver.
    c. heart.
    d. crop.

_______**19.** The structure labeled *C* is the
    a. gizzard.
    b. liver.
    c. heart.
    d. crop.

_______**20.** The structure responsible for kneading and crushing food is labeled
    a. *A.*
    b. *B.*
    c. *C.*
    d. *D.*

Name _________________________________ Class _______________ Date _____________

Chapter Test

Reptiles and Birds

In the space provided, write the letter of the description that best matches the term or phrase.

_______ **1.** uric acid

_______ **2.** albumen

_______ **3.** pectoral girdle

_______ **4.** barbule

_______ **5.** wishbone

_______ **6.** gizzard

a. form of nitrogenous waste excreted by a bird

b. chamber of a bird's stomach where food is crushed

c. one of the projections on the branches of a contour feather

d. bones that supports the forelimb bones

e. source of protein and water for the embryo in an amniotic egg

f. fused collarbones of a bird

In the space provided, write the letter of the term or phrase that best completes each statement or best answers each question.

_______ **7.** A female alligator usually does all of the following EXCEPT
   a. build a nest of rotting vegetation for her eggs.
   b. abandon her eggs after she lays them.
   c. tear open the nest to free the hatchlings.
   d. protect the young alligators for up to a year.

_______ **8.** What is the function of a bird's air sacs?
   a. to allow one-way air flow through the lungs
   b. to help provide lift during flight
   c. to increase the buoyancy of diving birds
   d. to provide additional area for gas exchange

_______ **9.** The geographical range of reptiles is limited mainly because reptiles
   a. cannot move easily on land.
   b. cannot swim or survive in water.
   c. live in a very limited variety of habitats.
   d. generally cannot function in cold environments.

_______ **10.** A short, thick, strong beak is usually found on birds that
   a. sip nectar.
   b. spear fish.
   c. crack seeds.
   d. probe for insects.

❙ Chapter Test *continued*

_______**11.** For a reptile that lives on land, internal fertilization is an important
adaptation because it
   a. protects the gametes from predators.
   b. protects the gametes from drying out.
   c. ensures that both parents are of the same species.
   d. ensures that both parents will care for the offspring.

_______**12.** In the heart of most reptiles, oxygen-rich and oxygen-poor blood
   a. mix completely in the atria.
   b. mix completely in the ventricle.
   c. mix somewhat in the ventricle.
   d. remain completely separate in the ventricle.

Complete each statement by writing the correct term or phrase in the space provided.

13. Crocodilians are the only reptiles that have a heart with a completely divided

_______________________ .

14. Reptiles are _____________________ , which are animals that warm their
bodies by absorbing heat from their environment.

15. Like reptiles, birds lay _____________________ eggs and have

_____________________ on their legs and feet.

16. Numerous internal _____________________ greatly increase the respiratory

surface area of a reptile's lungs, and strong _____________________

attached to the rib cage add to the lungs' efficiency.

17. Rattlesnakes inject venom into their prey through hollow upper front teeth

called _____________________ .

18. The body of an adult bird is covered by _____________________

_____________________ , which give the birds their shape.

19. The lower (ventral) portion of a tortoise's shell is called the

_____________________ .

20. In birds, the _____________________ have been modified into wings.

| Chapter Test *continued*

Read each question, and write your answer in the space provided.

21. What beak and foot adaptations help birds of prey feed?

____

____

____

22. Explain how the unique jaw structure of snakes helps snakes feed.

____

____

____

23. Name two types of feathers, and describe their functions.

____

____

____

____

____

24. What is a pit organ, and how does it benefit a rattlesnake?

____

____

____

____

____

25. Trace the circulation of blood through the heart of a bird.

____

____

____

____

____

____

Data Lab

Identifying Ectotherms

Background

The body temperature of all animals changes during the course of a day. How it changes can help you identify an animal as an ectotherm or an endotherm.

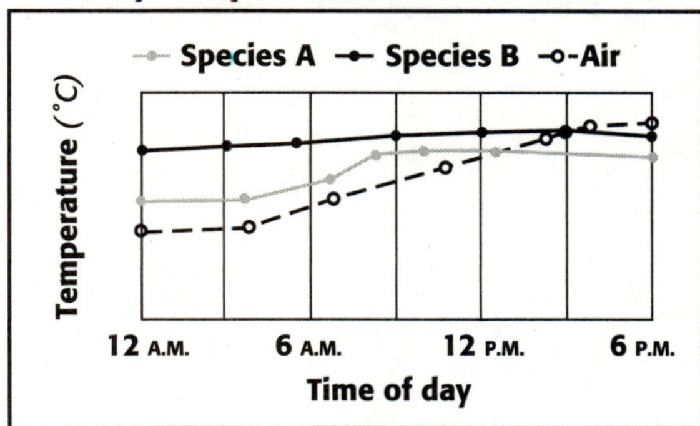

Analysis

1. Analyze the data and determine which animal species, A or B, is most likely an ectotherm. Explain your reasoning.

____

____

____

2. Identify the time of day the animal you identified as an ectotherm reaches its lowest body temperature.

____

3. Identify the time of day the animal you identified as an ectotherm reaches its highest body temperature.

____

4. Propose a reason why the ectotherm's body temperature is highest at this time.

____

5. Predict what the endotherm's graph line would look like if it were extended to show body temperature between 6 P.M. and midnight.

____

____

Modeling Watertight Skin

Modeling Watertight Skin

Scales make a reptile's skin almost watertight. This is one of reptiles' adaptations to terrestrial life. You can use grapes to model and compare water loss in different types of skin.

MATERIALS

- forceps
- 2 grapes
- balance
- Petri dish

Procedure

1. Find the mass of one grape, and record it in the data table. Then place the grape in an open Petri dish.

2. Using forceps, peel the skin from the second grape. Find and record the mass of the peeled grape. Then place it in the same Petri dish, but do not let the two grapes touch.

3. Wait 15 minutes, and then find and record the mass of each grape again.

<table>
<tr><th colspan="3">Data Table</th></tr>
<tr><td></td><th>Grape</th><th>Peeled Grape</th></tr>
<tr><td>Initial Mass</td><td></td><td></td></tr>
<tr><td>Mass after 15 minutes</td><td></td><td></td></tr>
</table>

Analysis

1. **Calculate** the difference between the original and final masses of each grape.

____

____

2. **Propose** an explanation for any changes in mass you observed.

____

____

____

| Modeling Watertight Skin *continued*

3. Determine which grape represents an amphibian's skin and which represents a reptile's skin.

____

____

4. Describe how a watertight skin is an adaptation to terrestrial life. Include information you have learned in this lab in your explanation.

____

____

____

____

Math Lab

DATASHEET FOR IN-TEXT LAB

Calculating Average Bone Density

Background

Density is the ratio of the mass of an object to its volume. Several teams of students determined the density of bones from two different animals. You can use their data to practice calculating average bone density.

1. Add the densities of one bone type. For example, if three bone samples

Data Table

Bone type	Team 1	Team 2	Team 3	Team 4
Animal 1	1.6 g/cm^3	1.0 g/cm^3	1.2 g/cm^3	1.4 g/cm^3
Animal 2	2.3 g/cm^3	1.8 g/cm^3	1.8 g/cm^3	2.1 g/cm^3

have densities of 3.0, 3.1, and 2.9 g/cm^3, their sum would be 9.0 g/cm^3.

2. Divide the sum of the densities by the number of samples.

$$\text{Average density} = \frac{\text{sum of the densities}}{\text{number of samples}} = \frac{9.0 \text{g/cm}^3}{3} = 3.0 \text{g/cm}^3$$

Analysis

1. Calculate the average bone density for each of the two animals in the data table. Express your answer in grams per cubic centimeter.

____

2. Critical Thinking
Evaluating Methods Why is it important to analyze several samples and obtain the average of your data?

____

____

3. Critical Thinking
Drawing Conclusions Based on your answer to item 1, which of the two animals is more likely to be a bird?

____

____

Observing Color Change in Anoles

SKILLS

- Using scientific methods
- Observing

OBJECTIVES

- **Observe** live anoles.
- **Relate** the color of an anole to the color of its surroundings.

MATERIALS

- glass-marking pencil
- 2 large, clear jars with wide mouths and lids with air holes
- 2 live anoles
- 6 shades each of brown and green construction paper, ranging from light to dark (2 swatches of each shade)

Before You Begin

Lizards are a group of **reptiles.** There are 250–300 species of anoles, lizards in the genus *Anolis.* Like chameleons, anoles can change color, ranging from brown to green. Anoles live in shrubs, grasses, and trees. Light level, temperature, and other factors, such as whether the animal is frightened or has eaten recently, can all affect the color of an anole. When anoles are frightened, they usually turn dark gray or brown and are unlikely to respond to other **stimuli.** Anoles generally change color within a few minutes. In this lab, you will observe the ability of anoles to change color when they are placed on different background colors. You will also determine how this ability might be an advantage to anoles.

1. Write a definition for each boldface term in the paragraph above.

____

____

____

____

2. You will be using the data table provided to record your data.

3. Based on the objectives for this lab, write a question you would like to explore about the color-changing behavior of anoles.

____

____

Observing Color Change in Anoles *continued*

Procedure
PART A: MAKE OBSERVATIONS

1. Observe live anoles in a terrarium. Make a list of characteristics that indicate that anoles are reptiles.

____

____

2.  Work with a partner to place anoles to be studied in separate glass jars. **CAUTION: Handle anoles gently, and follow instructions carefully. Anoles run fast and are easily frightened. Plan your actions before you start.** By working efficiently, you can keep your anole from becoming overly frightened. Carefully pick up one anole by grasping it firmly but gently around the shoulders. Do not pick up anoles by their tail. Place the anole in a glass jar. Quickly and carefully place a lid with air holes on the jar.

3. When anoles become overly frightened, they remain dark. While you are designing your experiment, do not disturb your anoles, and let them recover from your handling.

PART B: DESIGN AN EXPERIMENT

4. Work with members of your lab group to explore one of the questions written for step 3 of **Before You Begin.** To explore the question, design an experiment that uses the materials listed for this lab.

> **You Choose**
>
> As you design your experiment, decide the following:
>
> **a.** what question you will explore
>
> **b.** what hypothesis you will test
>
> **c.** how many anoles you will need
>
> **d.** what background colors you will use
>
> **e.** how many times you will test each background with an anole
>
> **f.** how long you will observe each test and how you will keep track of time
>
> **g.** what your control will be
>
> **h.** what data to record in your data table

Observing Color Change in Anoles *continued*

5. Write a procedure for your experiment. Make a list of all the safety precautions you will take. Have your teacher approve your procedure and safety precautions before you begin the experiment.

Data Table

Anole	Color 1		Color 2	
	Change	Time	Change	Time
1				
2				

6. Set up and carry out your experiment.

PART C: CLEANUP AND DISPOSAL

7.  Dispose of construction paper and broken glass in the designated waste containers. Put anoles in the designated container. Do not put lab materials in the trash unless your teacher tells you to do so.

8. Clean up your work area and all lab equipment. Return lab equipment to its proper place. Wash your hands thoroughly before you leave the lab.

Analyze and Conclude

1. Summarizing Results Briefly state how the variable you tested influenced the color-changing behavior of anoles.

____

____

____

2. Evaluating Results Did any unplanned variables influence your data? (For example, was there a loud noise, or was a jar suddenly moved?)

____

____

____

3. Analyzing Methods How could your experiment be modified to improve the certainty of your results?

____

____

____

Observing Color Change in Anoles *continued*

4. **Analyzing Data** Were there any inconsistencies in your data? (For example, two anoles reacted in different ways.) If so, offer an explanation for them.

____

____

____

5. **Drawing Conclusions** After considering your data, make a statement about color-changing behavior in anoles.

____

____

____

6. **Further Inquiry** Write a new question about anoles that could be explored with another investigation.

____

____

____

Using a Dichotomous Key to Identify Lizards

Imagine that you've just found a plant or an animal that you've never seen before. If you're like most people, one of the first questions you would ask is "What kind is it?" One way to answer that question is to thumb through the pages of a field guide, looking for an illustration that matches the organism you've found.

A more systematic way to identify an unknown organism is to use a dichotomous key. *Dichotomous* means "to divide into two parts." A dichotomous key consists of pairs of statements that usually pertain to the external features of the organism. The two statements in each pair are mutually exclusive, so they divide the possible choices in two. For example, a dichotomous key for identifying trees might begin with the following pair of statements:

   1.   Leaves scalelike or needlelike..2
       Leaves broad..14

If the first statement in pair 1 was correct for the tree in question, the key would direct you to the second pair of statements:

   2.   Leaves scalelike, concealing the twigs.............................3
       Leaves needlelike, not concealing the twigs......................4

Conversely, if the second statement in pair 1 was correct, the key would direct you to a later pair of statements:

  14. Bark peeling...15
       Bark not peeling..16

By carefully considering each statement and following the directions in the key, you can eventually identify the organism.

In this lab, you will use a dichotomous key to identify seven genera of lizards that are found in the western United States.

OBJECTIVES

Distinguish between seven genera of lizards on the basis of their external features.

Identify each genus of lizard by using a dichotomous key.

MATERIALS

- pencil or pen
- sheet of paper

Procedure

1. Examine the dichotomous key shown on the next page. Read the two statements in pair 1 of the key.

Using a Dichotomous Key to Identify Lizards *continued*

2. Decide which statement in the pair is correct for the lizard shown in illustration A of **Figure 1.** If the correct statement is followed by a genus name, write the name in **Table 1.** If the correct statement is followed by a number, move to that number and read the two statements that follow it.

DICHOTOMOUS KEY TO LIZARDS OF THE WESTERN UNITED STATES

1. Scales rounded, very smooth and shiny all over body ....genus *Eumeces* (skinks)
    Scales not rounded all over body 2

2. Horns at back of head; usually 1 or 2 rows of enlarged fringe scales on side of body ....genus *Phrynosoma* (horned lizards)
    No horns or fringe scales...3

3. Large, square scales on back and belly separated by a fold on side of body ....genus *Elgaria* (alligator lizards)
    No fold on side of body separating square back and belly scales 4

4. Fourth and fifth toes on hind limb about same length; tail stout, much shorter than body.......................................genus *Heloderma* (Gila monster)
    Fourth toe on hind limb much longer than fifth; tail as long as or longer than body, not stout...5

5. Back scales small; belly scales much larger and arranged in straight rows...genus *Cnemidophorus* (whiptails)
    Back and belly scales not very different in size 6

6. A single row of enlarged scales down middle of back and tail...genus *Dipsosaurus* (desert iguana)
    No row of enlarged scales down middle of back and tail.............................7

7. All scales on back pointed, with ridge along middle of each scale ....genus *Sceloporus* (spiny lizards)
    Scales on back small, not pointed...other genera

---

3. Repeat step 2 until you arrive at the genus name of the lizard.

4. Record the identity of the lizard in **Table 1.**

5. Repeat steps 1–4 for the lizards shown in B–G of **Figure 1.**

Using a Dichotomous Key to Identify Lizards *continued*

FIGURE 1 SOME LIZARDS OF WESTERN UNITED STATES

| Using a Dichotomous Key to Identify Lizards *continued*

TABLE 1 IDENTITY OF LIZARDS

A		E	
B		F	
C		G	
D			

Analysis

Classifying Which lizards shown in **Figure 1** have hind limbs in which the fourth toe is much longer than the fifth? Identify these lizards by their genus names.

____

____

Conclusions

1. **Drawing Conclusions** What external features are useful for identifying lizards of the western United States?

   ____

   ____

   ____

   ____

   ____

2. **Evaluating Methods** What additional information or materials would have helped you identify the lizards, using the dichotomous key?

   ____

   ____

Extension

Research and Communications Investigate the lizards that are found in your area. Identify each species, and list its habitat preferences and feeding habits. Describe how the activity levels of the lizards vary throughout the year. Report your findings in a poster or an illustrated written report.

Conducting a Bird Survey

Environmental factors such as climate changes, habitat disruption, and pollution can change the distribution of plant and animal populations. Severe environmental alterations may even cause some species to disappear completely from an area. Those species may be replaced by others that are better adapted to the altered environment. To know whether such population changes are taking place, it is important to carefully survey the populations in question.

Birds are good indicators of the health of the environment. They are also relatively easy to survey, for several reasons. Most birds are active during the daytime, and one of their characteristic activities—flying—often makes birds easy to spot. A wealth of information is available about the appearance, behavior, and seasonal distribution of each species. As a result, even inexperienced bird watchers can quickly identify many species through careful observation.

In this lab, you will study six species of birds that live in your area. You will observe a variety of characteristics of the birds and use those characteristics to identify each species.

OBJECTIVES

Observe birds in a particular area.

Describe each bird's physical characteristics and behaviors.

Identify each bird by using a field guide.

MATERIALS

- binoculars
- bird observation forms (6 copies)
- camera (optional)
- clipboard
- field guide to birds
- pencil
- watch

Procedure

1. Obtain 6 copies of the bird observation form on the next page.

2. Go to the area where you will make your observations. Be sure to bring all of the items in the materials list above.

3. When you spot a bird in your observation area, record the time on one of your observation forms.

4. Do not immediately try to identify the bird by looking in your field guide. (While you're searching through the guide, the bird may fly away.) Instead, carefully observe the bird's physical characteristics. Pay attention to the bird's color and markings, as well as to the shape and size of its wings, neck, bill, and tail. Also note the position of the bird's legs during flight. Record your observations on the form by checking the appropriate boxes and filling in the blanks.

Conducting a Bird Survey *continued*

BIRD OBSERVATION FORM

Names of observers: ____

Date: ____ Time: ________________________

Location of sighting: ____

Species: ____

Physical characteristics

Color and markings: ____

____

Wings:	❏ Pointed (outermost feathers longest)
	❏ Rounded (middle feathers longest)
	❏ Slotted (every other feather stands out)
Bill:	❏ Longer than the head
	❏ The same length as or shorter than the head
Neck:	❏ Longer than the body
	❏ The same length as or shorter than the body
Tail:	❏ Longer than the body
	❏ The same length as or shorter than the body
	❏ Square (all tail feathers the same length)
	❏ Rounded (feathers successively longer toward the center)
	❏ Pointed (middle feathers much longer than the others)
	❏ Forked (feathers increase in length from the middle out)
Legs:	❏ Extended beyond the body in flight
	❏ Drawn under the body in flight

Behavior

Alone:	❏ With other birds Number of birds in group ________________
Feeding:	❏ While walking
	❏ While flying
	Type of food eaten ____

Nest

❏ Shaped like a hollow sphere

❏ Shaped like an elongated sac

❏ Large, flat

❏ Shallow, on the ground

❏ At the end of a burrow below the ground

❏ In a cavity in a tree or limb

❏ In a crevice in a cliff or wall

Conducting a Bird Survey *continued*

5. Note whether the bird is alone or with other birds. If it is with others, count or estimate the number of birds in the group. Record your observations on the form.

6. If the bird you are observing is in a nest, record the type of nest and its location on the form.

7. Try to make a visual representation of the bird by photographing or videotaping it or by drawing it on the back of the form.

8. After you have finished entering your observations, find the bird in your field guide. If you think you know what bird it is, look it up in the guide's index. If you have no idea what kind of bird it is, thumb through the guide until you find a section with birds that look similar to the one you observed. Then carefully go through that section to find the correct species.

9. Notice that for each species, the guide includes an illustration or a photograph, a verbal description of the bird's appearance and behavior, and a map showing its approximate geographic range. The maps typically use different colors or patterns to indicate ranges that vary with the seasons.

10. Compare your notes on the bird and your visual representation of it with the illustrations, verbal descriptions, and range maps for similar-looking species. When you find a match, enter on the form the scientific and common names of the species.

11. Record on the form the location where the bird was observed.

12. Repeat steps 3–11 for five other bird species.

Analysis

1. Classifying Field guides typically place related species of birds in general groups. For example, the blackpoll warbler and American redstart may be placed in a group called wood-warblers, and the merlin and American kestrel may be classified as falcons. List the birds you observed according to the general types that are recognized in the field guide you used.

____

____

____

2. Analyzing Results What general types of birds did you observe most often?

____

____

____

____

Conducting a Bird Survey *continued*

Conclusions

1. Evaluating Methods Why is it important to base the identification of a bird on several factors, including various physical characteristics and behaviors?

____

____

____

____

____

2. Defending Conclusions A person in Salt Lake City, Utah, observes a bird that has yellow feathers on its undersides and in front of its eyes and a black, V-shaped band on its breast. Its bill is slightly shorter than its head, which has four dark bands that extend from front to back. The feathers on the back and the tops of the wings are mottled brown and black. The student concludes that the bird is an eastern meadowlark. Is that conclusion likely to be correct? Explain why or why not.

____

____

____

____

____

Extensions

1. Designing Experiments Develop a procedure to determine whether different species of birds are found in your area during different seasons, or whether the same species show different behaviors during different seasons.

2. Research and Communications Research bird surveys that have been conducted in your area in previous years. Find out whether populations of certain bird species appear to be declining or increasing. Report the results of your research in a short paper or an oral presentation.

Name _______________________ Class ______________ Date ______________

(Data Lab)

Identifying Ectotherms

Background

The body temperature of all animals changes during the course of a day. How it changes can help you identify an animal as an ectotherm or an endotherm.

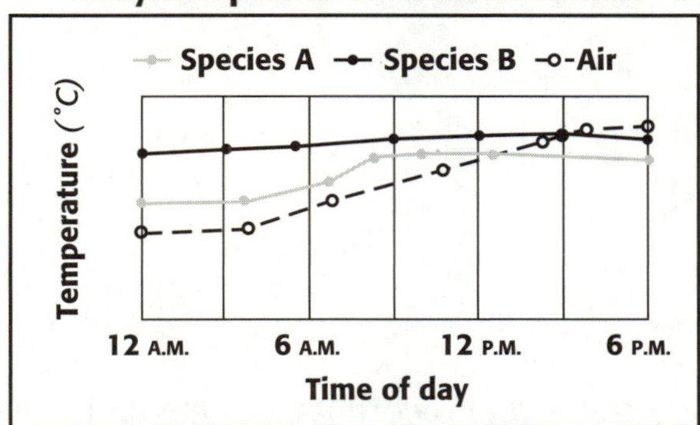

Analysis

1. **Analyze** the data and determine which animal species, A or B, is most likely an ectotherm. Explain your reasoning.

   Species A (gray curve) probably is an ectotherm. Its temperature increases

   during the day, when the air temperature increases.

2. **Identify** the time of day the animal you identified as an ectotherm reaches its lowest body temperature.

   around 12 A.M.

3. **Identify** the time of day the animal you identified as an ectotherm reaches its highest body temperature.

   around 12 P.M.

4. **Propose** a reason why the ectotherm's body temperature is highest at this time.

   It has been exposed to sunlight-warmed air since early in the morning.

5. **Predict** what the endotherm's graph line would look like if it were extended to show body temperature between 6 p.m. and midnight.

   It would decline steadily from its value at 6 P.M. to its value at 12 A.M.

Name _________________________________ Class ______________ Date ______________

DATASHEET FOR IN-TEXT LAB

Modeling Watertight Skin

Modeling Watertight Skin

Scales make a reptile's skin almost watertight. This is one of reptiles' adaptations to terrestrial life. You can use grapes to model and compare water loss in different types of skin.

MATERIALS

- forceps
- 2 grapes
- balance
- Petri dish

Procedure

1. Find the mass of one grape, and record it in a data table. Then place the grape in an open Petri dish.

2. Using forceps, peel the skin from the second grape. Find and record the mass of the peeled grape. Then place it in the same Petri dish, but do not let the two grapes touch.

3. Wait 15 minutes, and then find and record the mass of each grape again.

Data Table		
	Grape	**Peeled Grape**
Initial Mass		
Mass after 15 minutes		

Analysis

1. Calculate the difference between the original and final masses of each grape.

The mass of the skinless grape should decrease. The mass of the intact grape should stay the same.

2. Propose an explanation for any changes in mass you observed.

The skin prevents water from evaporating from an intact grape, so the grape's weight does not change. Without its skin, a grape loses water and becomes lighter.

Name _______________________________ Class _______________ Date _____________

Modeling Watertight Skin *continued*

3. Determine which grape represents an amphibian's skin and which represents a reptile's skin.

The skinless grape represents an amphibian's skin. The intact grape

represents a reptile's skin.

4. Describe how a watertight skin is an adaptation to terrestrial life. Include information you have learned in this lab in your explanation.

Watertight skin, as in the intact grape, prevents water loss. This allows an

animal to survive in dry environments. Most amphibians, like the skinless

grape, would dry up if out of water or a moist environment for an extended

period of time.

Name _______________________________ Class _______________ Date _____________

DATASHEET FOR IN-TEXT LAB

Calculating Average Bone Density

Background

Density is the ratio of the mass of an object to its volume. Several teams of students determined the density of bones from two different animals. You can use their data to practice calculating average bone density.

Data Table				
Bone type	**Team 1**	**Team 2**	**Team 3**	**Team 4**
Animal 1	1.6 g/cm^3	1.0 g/cm^3	1.2 g/cm^3	1.4 g/cm^3
Animal 2	2.3 g/cm^3	1.8 g/cm^3	1.8 g/cm^3	2.1 g/cm^3

1. **Add the densities of one bone type.** For example, if three bone samples have densities of 3.0, 3.1, and 2.9 g/cm^3, their sum would be 9.0 g/cm^3.

$$\text{Average density} = \frac{\text{sum of the densities}}{\text{number of samples}} = \frac{9.0 \text{g/cm}^3}{3} = 3.0 \text{g/cm}^3$$

2. **Divide the sum of the densities by the number of samples.**

Analysis

1. **Calculate** the average bone density for each of the two animals in the data table. Express your answer in grams per cubic centimeter.

   Animal 1: 1.3 g/cm^3; Animal 2: 2.0 g/cm^3

2. **Critical Thinking**
   Evaluating Methods Why is it important to analyze several samples and obtain the average of your data?

   A certain amount of variation is normal in biological systems.

3. **Critical Thinking**
   Drawing Conclusions Based on your answer to item 1, which of the two animals is more likely to be a bird?

   Animal 1

Name _______________________________ Class _______________ Date ___________

(Exploration Lab)

Observing Color Change in Anoles

SKILLS

- Using scientific methods
- Observing

OBJECTIVES

- **Observe** live anoles.
- **Relate** the color of an anole to the color of its surroundings.

MATERIALS

- glass-marking pencil
- 2 large, clear jars with wide mouths and lids with air holes
- 2 live anoles
- 6 shades each of brown and green construction paper, ranging from light to dark (2 swatches of each shade)

Before You Begin

Lizards are a group of **reptiles.** There are 250–300 species of anoles, lizards in the genus *Anolis.* Like chameleons, anoles can change color, ranging from brown to green. Anoles live in shrubs, grasses, and trees. Light level, temperature, and other factors, such as whether the animal is frightened or has eaten recently, can all affect the color of an anole. When anoles are frightened, they usually turn dark gray or brown and are unlikely to respond to other **stimuli.** Anoles generally change color within a few minutes. In this lab, you will observe the ability of anoles to change color when they are placed on different background colors. You will also determine how this ability might be an advantage to anoles.

1. Write a definition for each boldface term in the paragraph above.

reptiles—**ectothermic vertebrates with scaly, watertight skin; lungs; and a**

heart with partially or completely divided ventricle.

stimuli—**environmental factors that influence the behavior of an organism**

____

2. You will be using the data table provided to record your data.

3. Based on the objectives for this lab, write a question you would like to explore about the color-changing behavior of anoles.

Answers will vary. For example: How quickly do anoles change color after

they move to a new background color?

Name _______________________________ Class ______________ Date ______________

Observing Color Change in Anoles *continued*

Procedure

PART A: MAKE OBSERVATIONS

1. Observe live anoles in a terrarium. Make a list of characteristics that indicate that anoles are reptiles.

Easily observed characteristics include scaly skin and toes with claws.

2.  Work with a partner to place anoles to be studied in separate glass jars. **CAUTION: Handle anoles gently, and follow instructions carefully. Anoles run fast and are easily frightened. Plan your actions before you start.** By working efficiently, you can keep your anole from becoming overly frightened. Carefully pick up one anole by grasping it firmly but gently around the shoulders. Do not pick up anoles by their tail. Place the anole in a glass jar. Quickly and carefully place a lid with air holes on the jar.

3. When anoles become overly frightened, they remain dark. While you are designing your experiment, do not disturb your anoles, and let them recover from your handling.

PART B: DESIGN AN EXPERIMENT

4. Work with members of your lab group to explore one of the questions written for step 3 of **Before You Begin.** To explore the question, design an experiment that uses the materials listed for this lab.

> **You Choose**
>
> As you design your experiment, decide the following:
>
> **a.** what question you will explore
>
> **b.** what hypothesis you will test
>
> **c.** how many anoles you will need
>
> **d.** what background colors you will use
>
> **e.** how many times you will test each background with an anole
>
> **f.** how long you will observe each test and how you will keep track of time
>
> **g.** what your control will be
>
> **h.** what data to record in your data table

Name _________________________________ Class ________________ Date ______________

| Observing Color Change in Anoles *continued*

5. Write a procedure for your experiment. Make a list of all the safety precautions you will take. Have your teacher approve your procedure and safety precautions before you begin the experiment.

	Data Table			
	Color 1		**Color 2**	
Anole	**Change**	**Time**	**Change**	**Time**
1				
2				

6. Set up and carry out your experiment.

PART C: CLEANUP AND DISPOSAL

7.  Dispose of construction paper and broken glass in the designated waste containers. Put anoles in the designated container. Do not put lab materials in the trash unless your teacher tells you to do so.

8. Clean up your work area and all lab equipment. Return lab equipment to its proper place. Wash your hands thoroughly before you leave the lab.

Analyze and Conclude

1. Summarizing Results Briefly state how the variable you tested influenced the color-changing behavior of anoles.

Students' answers should clearly describe how each test was conducted and should state their results in terms of color changes in the anoles. See Sample Data Table in the TE for this lab.

2. Evaluating Results Did any unplanned variables influence your data? (For example, was there a loud noise, or was a jar suddenly moved?)

Anoles may react to stimuli other than the independent variable selected. Students may list several uncontrolled variables, such as temperature or environmental stressors, which could have affected their results.

3. Analyzing Methods How could your experiment be modified to improve the certainty of your results?

Answers will depend on the groups' experimental designs. Students should suggest improving their methods by eliminating or controlling as many uncontrolled variables as possible.

Name _______________________________ Class _______________ Date _______________

Observing Color Change in Anoles *continued*

4. **Analyzing Data** Were there any inconsistencies in your data? (For example, two anoles reacted in different ways.) If so, offer an explanation for them.

Answers will vary. Students should include a possible explanation for any inconsistency observed.

5. **Drawing Conclusions** After considering your data, make a statement about color-changing behavior in anoles.

Answers will vary. For example: Anoles change to a color that most closely matches the color of their environment.

6. **Further Inquiry** Write a new question about anoles that could be explored with another investigation.

Answers will vary. For example: Would anoles react differently if there were two in each jar?

　　　　　　　　　　　　　　　　　OBSERVATION

Using a Dichotomous Key to Identify Lizards

Teacher Notes

TIME REQUIRED One 45-minute period

SKILLS ACQUIRED
Classifying
Identifying and recognizing patterns
Interpreting

RATINGS　　　　Easy ◄——1——2——3——4——► Hard
Teacher Prep–1
Student Setup–1
Concept Level–2
Cleanup–1

THE SCIENTIFIC METHOD

Make Observations Students must observe illustrations carefully as they work through a dichotomous key.

Draw Conclusions Conclusions question 1 asks students to draw conclusions from their classification.

TIPS AND TRICKS

This lab works best in groups of two students but can be done individually.

Explain that the toes on the hind limbs of a lizard are numbered from 1 (at the front, close to the body) to 5 (at the rear, close to the body). The first toe is equivalent to the big toe of a human. Have students study illustration C of Figure 1 as you explain the numbering convention.

If students are unfamiliar with a dichotomous key, you may want to introduce it to them by comparing it to a game of Twenty Questions. In that game, one player thinks of a specific person or thing, and the other players try to deduce the identity of the person or thing by asking questions that have two possible answers: yes or no. The answer to each question helps the other players decide what to ask next. Similarly, in a dichotomous key, the response to each statement determines the next statement to consider.

Name _______________________________ Class ______________ Date ____________

OBSERVATION

Using a Dichotomous Key to Identify Lizards

Imagine that you've just found a plant or an animal that you've never seen before. If you're like most people, one of the first questions you would ask is "What kind is it?" One way to answer that question is to thumb through the pages of a field guide, looking for an illustration that matches the organism you've found.

A more systematic way to identify an unknown organism is to use a dichotomous key. *Dichotomous* means "to divide into two parts." A dichotomous key consists of pairs of statements that usually pertain to the external features of the organism. The two statements in each pair are mutually exclusive, so they divide the possible choices in two. For example, a dichotomous key for identifying trees might begin with the following pair of statements:

1. Leaves scalelike or needlelike...2
   Leaves broad..14

If the first statement in pair 1 was correct for the tree in question, the key would direct you to the second pair of statements:

2. Leaves scalelike, concealing the twigs..3
   Leaves needlelike, not concealing the twigs 4

Conversely, if the second statement in pair 1 was correct, the key would direct you to a later pair of statements:

14. Bark peeling..15
    Bark not peeling..16

By carefully considering each statement and following the directions in the key, you can eventually identify the organism.

In this lab, you will use a dichotomous key to identify seven genera of lizards that are found in the western United States.

OBJECTIVES

Distinguish between seven genera of lizards on the basis of their external features.

Identify each genus of lizard by using a dichotomous key.

MATERIALS

- pencil or pen
- sheet of paper

Procedure

1. Examine the dichotomous key shown on the next page. Read the two statements in pair 1 of the key.

Name _______________________________ Class _______________ Date ______________

Using a Dichotomous Key to Identify Lizards *continued*

2. Decide which statement in the pair is correct for the lizard shown in illustration A of **Figure 1.** If the correct statement is followed by a genus name, write the name in **Table 1.** If the correct statement is followed by a number, move to that number and read the two statements that follow it.

DICHOTOMOUS KEY TO LIZARDS OF THE WESTERN UNITED STATES

1. Scales rounded, very smooth and shiny all over body ....
    ....genus *Eumeces* (skinks)
    Scales not rounded all over body 2

2. Horns at back of head; usually 1 or 2 rows of enlarged fringe scales on
    side of body...genus *Phrynosoma* (horned lizards)
    No horns or fringe scales...3

3. Large, square scales on back and belly separated by a fold on side of body
    ....genus *Elgaria* (alligator lizards)
    No fold on side of body separating square back and belly scales 4

4. Fourth and fifth toes on hind limb about same length; tail stout, much
    shorter than body...................................genus *Heloderma* (Gila monster)
    Fourth toe on hind limb much longer than fifth; tail as long as or longer
    than body, not stout..5

5. Back scales small; belly scales much larger and arranged in straight rows...
    ....genus *Cnemidophorus* (whiptails)
    Back and belly scales not very different in size 6

6. A single row of enlarged scales down middle of back and tail.......................
    ....genus *Dipsosaurus* (desert iguana)
    No row of enlarged scales down middle of back and tail.............................7

7. All scales on back pointed, with ridge along middle of each scale ....
    ....genus *Sceloporus* (spiny lizards)
    Scales on back small, not pointed..other genera

---

3. Repeat step 2 until you arrive at the genus name of the lizard.

4. Record the identity of the lizard in **Table 1.**

5. Repeat steps 1–4 for the lizards shown in B–G of **Figure 1.**

Name _________________________________ Class _______________ Date _____________

Using a Dichotomous Key to Identify Lizards *continued*

FIGURE 1 SOME LIZARDS OF WESTERN UNITED STATES

Name _________________________________ Class _______________ Date ____________

Using a Dichotomous Key to Identify Lizards *continued*

TABLE 1 IDENTITY OF LIZARDS

A	*Sceloporus* (spiny lizard)	**E**	*Heloderma* (Gila monster)
B	*Elgaria* (alligator lizard)	**F**	*Dipsosaurus* (desert iguana)
C	*Cnemidophorus* (whiptail)	**G**	*Phrynosoma* (horned lizard)
D	*Eumeces* (skink)		

Analysis

Classifying Which lizards shown in **Figure 1** have hind limbs in which the fourth toe is much longer than the fifth? Identify these lizards by their genus names.

The lizards are *Cnemidophorus, Dipsosaurus,* and *Sceloporus*.

Conclusions

1. **Drawing Conclusions** What external features are useful for identifying lizards of the western United States?

   Answers will vary but should include several of the following: the type of scales

   (rounded, smooth, shiny, pointed, ridged), the presence of horns at the back of

   the head, the presence of fringe scales or a fold on the side of the body, the

   relative length of the fourth and fifth toes on the hind limbs, the stoutness and

   length of the tail, and the relative size of scales on the back and belly.

2. **Evaluating Methods** What additional information or materials would have helped you identify the lizards, using the dichotomous key?

   Answers will vary. Students may have benefited from actual specimens or

   from examples of the anatomical descriptions.

Extension

Research and Communications Investigate the lizards that are found in your area. Identify each species, and list its habitat preferences and feeding habits. Describe how the activity levels of the lizards vary throughout the year. Report your findings in a poster or an illustrated written report.

Skills Practice Lab

FIELD ACTIVITY

Conducting a Bird Survey

Teacher Notes

TIME REQUIRED Two 45-minute periods; Time requirement will vary if the lab is assigned as a long-term, out-of-class project.

SKILLS ACQUIRED

Classifying
Collecting data
Communicating
Inferring
Organizing and analyzing data

RATINGS

Easy ← 1   2   3   4 → Hard

Teacher Prep–1
Student Setup–1
Concept Level–1
Cleanup–1

THE SCIENTIFIC METHOD

Make Observations Students observe the physical characteristics and behaviors of several species of birds in their area.

Analyze the Results Analysis question 2 asks students to analyze their results.

Draw Conclusions Students must draw conclusions to answer Conclusions questions 1 and 2.

MATERIALS

Field guides can be purchased from any bookstore. Binoculars can be purchased from stores that sell sporting goods, outdoor gear, or photographic equipment.

SAFETY CAUTIONS

- Discuss all safety symbols and caution statements with students.

- Before students go into the field, discuss any dangerous organisms they might find and how they may avoid these organisms. Show students pictures of poison ivy and other plants to avoid.

- Encourage students to dress appropriately for field work. They should wear comfortable clothing, long pants, and sturdy shoes with closed toes.

- Remind students to bring sunglasses, sunscreen, rain gear, and insect repellent, as needed.

- Discuss field trip safety procedures. For example, have students remain within a distance that they can be seen or heard by you or other students. Assign students to work in pairs or small groups for additional safety.

Conducting a Bird Survey *continued*

TECHNIQUES TO DEMONSTRATE

You may want to demonstrate the proper technique of using binoculars. Students who have never used binoculars before may be unaware of how to focus them.

TIPS AND TRICKS

Preparation

This lab works best in groups of two or three students.

You may wish to present this lab as a two- or three-day field activity or as a longer-term, out-of-class project.

Prior to the start of the lab, meet with students and discuss where they will conduct their observations, such as on the school grounds or at a nearby park. If your observation area has a variety of habitats, you may wish to assign different groups to different habitats.

Have students read through the Procedure before going out into the field.

Some field guides are divided into separate volumes for western and eastern North America. Make sure the guides that students are using are appropriate for where they live. Suggest that students become familiar with the organization of the field guide and how to use it. From the guide, students should realize that male birds usually have more colorful markings than female birds.

You may want to make multiple copies of the bird observation form for students to use. If so, instruct students to skip step 1 in the Procedure.

Procedure

Students may not have a chance to collect all of the information listed on the bird observation form, such as that relating to flight, feeding, and nests. Tell students to indicate on each form which features they were unable to observe.

The procedure calls for each group of students to observe six species of birds. You may increase or decrease this number depending on the variety of local bird species and the amount of time students have to make their observations.

Encourage students to be aware of the impact they have on the areas where they make their observations. Remind students to leave the areas as they found them. Emphasize that they should not pick up any birds or eggs or touch any nests.

If time permits, have each group present their findings to the class so that all students can appreciate the variety of local bird species.

Name _______________________________ Class _______________ Date _____________

FIELD ACTIVITY

Conducting a Bird Survey

Environmental factors such as climate changes, habitat disruption, and pollution can change the distribution of plant and animal populations. Severe environmental alterations may even cause some species to disappear completely from an area. Those species may be replaced by others that are better adapted to the altered environment. To know whether such population changes are taking place, it is important to carefully survey the populations in question.

Birds are good indicators of the health of the environment. They are also relatively easy to survey, for several reasons. Most birds are active during the daytime, and one of their characteristic activities—flying—often makes birds easy to spot. A wealth of information is available about the appearance, behavior, and seasonal distribution of each species. As a result, even inexperienced bird watchers can quickly identify many species through careful observation.

In this lab, you will study six species of birds that live in your area. You will observe a variety of characteristics of the birds and use those characteristics to identify each species.

OBJECTIVES

Observe birds in a particular area.

Describe each bird's physical characteristics and behaviors.

Identify each bird by using a field guide.

MATERIALS

- binoculars
- bird observation forms (6 copies)
- camera (optional)
- clipboard
- field guide to birds
- pencil
- watch

Procedure

1. Obtain 6 copies of the bird observation form on the next page.

2. Go to the area where you will make your observations. Be sure to bring all of the items in the materials list above.

3. When you spot a bird in your observation area, record the time on one of your observation forms.

4. Do not immediately try to identify the bird by looking in your field guide. (While you're searching through the guide, the bird may fly away.) Instead, carefully observe the bird's physical characteristics. Pay attention to the bird's color and markings, as well as to the shape and size of its wings, neck, bill, and tail. Also note the position of the bird's legs during flight. Record your observations on the form by checking the appropriate boxes and filling in the blanks.

Name _______________________________ Class _______________ Date _______________

Conducting a Bird Survey *continued*

BIRD OBSERVATION FORM

Names of observers: ____

Date: ______________________________________ Time: ___________________

Location of sighting: ____

Species: ____

Physical characteristics

Color and markings: ____

____

Wings: ❑ Pointed (outermost feathers longest)

❑ Rounded (middle feathers longest)

❑ Slotted (every other feather stands out)

Bill: ❑ Longer than the head

❑ The same length as or shorter than the head

Neck: ❑ Longer than the body

❑ The same length as or shorter than the body

Tail: ❑ Longer than the body

❑ The same length as or shorter than the body

❑ Square (all tail feathers the same length)

❑ Rounded (feathers successively longer toward the center)

❑ Pointed (middle feathers much longer than the others)

❑ Forked (feathers increase in length from the middle out)

Legs: ❑ Extended beyond the body in flight

❑ Drawn under the body in flight

Behavior

Alone: ❑ With other birds   Number of birds in group _______________

Feeding: ❑ While walking

❑ While flying

Type of food eaten ____

Nest

❑ Shaped like a hollow sphere

❑ Shaped like an elongated sac

❑ Large, flat

❑ Shallow, on the ground

❑ At the end of a burrow below the ground

❑ In a cavity in a tree or limb

❑ In a crevice in a cliff or wall

Name _______________________________ Class _______________ Date _____________

Conducting a Bird Survey *continued*

5. Note whether the bird is alone or with other birds. If it is with others, count or estimate the number of birds in the group. Record your observations on the form.

6. If the bird you are observing is in a nest, record the type of nest and its location on the form.

7. Try to make a visual representation of the bird by photographing or videotaping it or by drawing it on the back of the form.

8. After you have finished entering your observations, find the bird in your field guide. If you think you know what bird it is, look it up in the guide's index. If you have no idea what kind of bird it is, thumb through the guide until you find a section with birds that look similar to the one you observed. Then carefully go through that section to find the correct species.

9. Notice that for each species, the guide includes an illustration or a photograph, a verbal description of the bird's appearance and behavior, and a map showing its approximate geographic range. The maps typically use different colors or patterns to indicate ranges that vary with the seasons.

10. Compare your notes on the bird and your visual representation of it with the illustrations, verbal descriptions, and range maps for similar-looking species. When you find a match, enter on the form the scientific and common names of the species.

11. Record on the form the location where the bird was observed.

12. Repeat steps 3–11 for five other bird species.

Analysis

1. **Classifying** Field guides typically place related species of birds in general groups. For example, the blackpoll warbler and American redstart may be placed in a group called wood-warblers, and the merlin and American kestrel may be classified as falcons. List the birds you observed according to the general types that are recognized in the field guide you used.

   Answers will vary. Check students' lists against the classification scheme

   presented in the field guide they used.

2. **Analyzing Results** What general types of birds did you observe most often?

   Answers will vary, depending in part on the locations where the observations

   were made. For example, ducks or wading birds may be most common near

   bodies of water, whereas sparrows may be most common in areas with trees

   and bushes.

Name _________________________________ Class _______________ Date _____________

Conducting a Bird Survey *continued*

Conclusions

1. **Evaluating Methods** Why is it important to base the identification of a bird on several factors, including various physical characteristics and behaviors?

   Possible answers include the following: Analyzing multiple factors gives a

   more complete characterization of the bird. Different species may have nearly

   identical physical characteristics but differ in behavior. Some physical charac-

   teristics or behaviors may not be observable because the bird did not assume

   the right posture or engage in certain activities. The bird may not show certain

   key physical characteristics because it is young or missing some feathers.

2. **Defending Conclusions** A person in Salt Lake City, Utah, observes a bird that has yellow feathers on its undersides and in front of its eyes and a black, V-shaped band on its breast. Its bill is slightly shorter than its head, which has four dark bands that extend from front to back. The feathers on the back and the tops of the wings are mottled brown and black. The student concludes that the bird is an eastern meadowlark. Is that conclusion likely to be correct? Explain why or why not.

   That conclusion is not likely to be correct. The physical characteristics

   match those of both the eastern meadowlark and the western meadowlark.

   However, the range maps for these species indicate that only the western

   meadowlark is found in Utah. Therefore, the bird that was observed probably

   was a western meadowlark.

Extensions

1. **Designing Experiments** Develop a procedure to determine whether different species of birds are found in your area during different seasons, or whether the same species show different behaviors during different seasons.

2. **Research and Communications** Research bird surveys that have been conducted in your area in previous years. Find out whether populations of certain bird species appear to be declining or increasing. Report the results of your research in a short paper or an oral presentation.

Answer Key

Directed Reading

SECTION: THE REPTILIAN BODY

1. with
2. ectothermic
3. watertight
4. birds
5. lungs
6. partly
7. internal
8. In very cold weather, most reptiles become sluggish and are unable to function. In temperate climates, they remain inactive through the winter.
9. The metabolism of reptiles does not generate enough heat to warm their bodies.
10. The legs of reptiles are positioned more directly under their bodies than are the limbs of amphibians.
11. b
12. c
13. d
14. a
15. In an oviparous animal, the young hatch from eggs that the female deposits in a suitable place. In an ovoviviparous animal, the female retains the eggs within her body until shortly before or after they hatch.
16. During internal fertilization, the eggs are fertilized within the female's body. During external fertilization, the eggs are fertilized outside of the female's body.

SECTION: TODAY'S REPTILES

1. Snakes and lizards have a lower jaw that is loosely connected to the skull.
2. Snakes and lizards have many similarities that point to a strong evolutionary relationship. Like several species of lizards, snakes lack moveable eyelids and external ears. Both snakes and lizards molt periodically.
3. Some snakes kill their prey by suffocation or by injecting lethal venom. Others seize their prey and swallow it whole.
4. cobras, kraits, and coral snakes; sea snakes; adders and vipers; and rattlesnakes, water moccasins, and copperheads
5. A pit organ is an organ that can detect infrared radiation. A timber rattlesnake uses its pit organs to locate warm-bodied animals in the cool nighttime, enabling the snake to hunt in total darkness.
6. Jacobson's organs are depressions in the roof of the snake's mouth that detect odors. The timber rattlesnake uses its Jacobson's organs to follow its prey's scent trail.
7. Having eyes high on the sides of their heads and nostrils on top of their snouts enables these animals to see and breathe while lying nearly submerged in the water.
8. Crocodilians care for their young after hatching. Other reptiles do not.
9. A tuatara is a lizardlike reptile that is native to New Zealand. Tuataras are active at low temperatures and feed at night.
10. Turtles generally live in water, while tortoises live on land.
11. The carapace is the top part of a turtle's shell. The plastron is the bottom portion of the shell.

SECTION: CHARACTERISTICS AND DIVERSITY OF BIRDS

1. forelimbs
2. scales
3. lightweight
4. endothermic
5. highly efficient
6. completely
7. Contour feathers cover a bird's body and give adult birds their shape. Down feathers cover the body of young birds and are found beneath the contour feathers of adults.
8. Preening reattaches the microscopic hooks that connect the barbs of a feather. Preening also spreads oil over a bird's feathers, which cleans and waterproofs them.

9. Birds' bones are hollow and thin.

10. Birds have a high rate of metabolism, which satisfies the increased energy requirements of flight.

11. The structure of a bird's lungs and the air sacs that connect to them create a one-way air flow through the bird's respiratory system.

12. Oxygen-rich and oxygen-poor blood are kept separate, enabling oxygen to be delivered to the cells more efficiently.

13. songbirds

14. hummingbirds

15. woodpeckers

16. parrots

17. birds of prey

18. ducks

19. long-legged waders

Active Reading

SECTION: THE REPTILIAN BODY

1. A reptile's body temperature is largely determined by the temperature of its environment.

2. The reptile's body temperature increases.

3. The lizard maintains a relatively constant body temperature.

4. a

SECTION: TODAY'S REPTILES

1. Other reptiles lack the protective shell that encases the body of a turtle or tortoise.

2. No; the shells of most tortoises are dome shaped, while most water-dwelling turtles have a streamlined, disk-shaped shell.

3. d

SECTION: CHARACTERISTICS AND DIVERSITY OF BIRDS

1. The lungs are exposed to almost fully oxygenated air, which increases the amount of oxygen transported to body cells. Because the flow of blood in the lungs runs in a different direction than the flow of air, oxygen absorption increases.

2. c

Vocabulary Review

1. b

2. e

3. d

4. a

5. c

6. down

7. contour

8. preen gland

Science Skills

APPLYING INFORMATION/ INTERPRETING TABLES

1. amniotic eggs, a cloaca, internal fertilization, and scales

2. ectothermic metabolism

3. feathers, wings, two legs, and endothermic metabolism

4. The existence of characteristics that are shared by reptiles and birds (amniotic eggs, a cloaca, internal fertilization, and scales) supports the proposal that birds and reptiles are similar enough to be grouped in the same class.

5. Birds have some characteristics, including feathers, wings, two legs, and endothermic metabolism, that reptiles lack. These differences suggest that birds and reptiles are dissimilar enough to be in different classes.

6. Answers may vary. Students may say that crocodilians and birds belong in the same class because both care for their young and have a completely divided heart ventricle. Alternatively, students may say that turtles and tortoises belong in the same class as birds because they all lack teeth.

Concept Mapping

1. metabolism

2. skeleton

3. ectothermic

4. solid bones or hollow bones

5. hollow bones or solid bones

6. internal folds or one-way air flow

7. one-way air flow or internal folds

8. feathers or scales

9. scales or feathers

10. hard shell or leathery shell

11. leathery shell or hard shell

Critical Thinking

1. c	**12.** a
2. d	**13.** c
3. a	**14.** l, f
4. b	**15.** c, j
5. f	**16.** e, h
6. c	**17.** b, d
7. d	**18.** i, k
8. a	**19.** a, g
9. e	**20.** d
10. b	**21.** b
11. b	**22.** d

Test Prep Pretest

1. c
2. d
3. a
4. c
5. b
6. b
7. c
8. a
9. d
10. ventricle, separate
11. hemotoxins
12. ducks
13. scales
14. ectotherms
15. amniotic, ancestor
16. oviparous
17. ovoviviparous
18. Chelonia—turtles; Rhynchocephalia—tuataras; Squamata—lizards and snakes; Crocodilia—crocodiles and alligators
19. A turtle's shell is streamlined and disk shaped.Depending on the species, the carapace (top) and plastron (bottom) are made of fused plates of bone covered with horny shields or tough, leathery skin. In most species, the vertebrae and ribs are fused to the inside of the carapace. The shell provides protection and support for muscle attachments.
20. A bird lung is more efficient. The lungs are connected to a series of air sacs that make one-way air flow possible. Thus, the lungs are exposed only to oxygenated air, which increases the amount of oxygen transported to the body cells. Also, because the flow of blood in the lungs runs in a different direction than the flow of air, oxygen absorption is increased.

Quiz

SECTION: THE REPTILIAN BODY

1. c	**6.** e
2. a	**7.** d
3. f	**8.** d
4. d	**9.** c
5. b	**10.** a

SECTION: TODAY'S REPTILES

1. d	**6.** b
2. a	**7.** b
3. e	**8.** c
4. f	**9.** a
5. c	**10.** c

SECTION: CHARACTERISTICS AND DIVERSITY OF BIRDS

1. a	**6.** c
2. f	**7.** d
3. d	**8.** c
4. b	**9.** b
5. e	**10.** a

Chapter Test (General)

1. f	**11.** d
2. b	**12.** d
3. a	**13.** a
4. g	**14.** c
5. d	**15.** a
6. e	**16.** b
7. c	**17.** b
8. c	**18.** d
9. b	**19.** a
10. c	**20.** c

Chapter Test (Advanced)

1. a	**7.** b
2. e	**8.** a
3. d	**9.** d
4. c	**10.** c
5. f	**11.** b
6. b	**12.** c

13. ventricle
14. ectotherms
15. amniotic, scales
16. folds, muscles
17. fangs
18. contour feathers

19. plastron

20. forelimbs

21. Birds of prey have curved, pointed beaks for tearing and pulling apart prey, and they have powerful, curved talons for seizing and gripping prey.

22. A snake's jaw is very flexible because it has five points of movement. At one of these points—the chin—the halves of the lower jaw are connected by an elastic ligament that permits the lower jaw to spread apart when a large meal is being swallowed.

23. Contour feathers cover an adult bird's body and give it shape. Specialized contour feathers on the wings and tail help provide lift for flight. Down feathers cover young birds and are found beneath the contour feathers of adults. Down feathers conserve body heat by providing insulation.

24. Pit organs are structures located between each eye and nostril of a rattlesnake, which can detect infrared radiation. They allow the snake to detect the difference in infrared radiation emitted by a warm-bodied animal and the cooler background. Thus, rattlesnakes can hunt in total darkness.

25. Oxygen-poor blood from the body enters the right atrium, which pumps this blood to the right ventricle. The right ventricle pumps the oxygen-poor blood to the lungs. Oxygen-rich blood from the lungs enters the left atrium, which pumps this blood to the left ventricle. The left ventricle pumps the oxygen-rich blood to the body.

Lesson Plan

Section: The Reptilian Body

Pacing

Regular Schedule: **with lab(s):** N/A **without lab(s):** 3 days

Block Schedule: **with lab(s):** N/A **without lab(s):** 1 1/2 days

Objectives

1. Describe the key characteristics of reptiles.

2. Relate a reptile's ectothermic metabolism to its activity level.

3. Summarize the adaptations that enable reptiles to live on land.

National Science Education Standards Covered

UNIFYING CONCEPTS AND PROCESSES

UCP1: Systems, order, and organization

UCP2: Evidence, models, and explanation

UCP5: Form and function

SCIENCE AS INQUIRY

SI1: Abilities necessary to do scientific inquiry

SI2: Understandings about scientific inquiry

LIFE SCIENCE: BIOLOGICAL EVOLUTION

LSEvol1: Species evolve over time.

LIFE SCIENCE: MATTER, ENERGY, AND ORGANIZATION IN LIVING SYSTEMS

LSMat4: The complexity and organization of organisms accommodates the need for obtaining, transforming, transporting, releasing, and eliminating the matter and energy used to sustain the organism.

LIFE SCIENCE: BEHAVIOR OF ORGANISMS

LSBeh2: Organisms have behavioral responses to internal changes and to external stimuli.

KEY

SE = Student Edition TE = Teacher Edition

CRF = Chapter Resource File

Block 1

CHAPTER OPENER *(45 minutes)*

_ **Quick Review,** SE. Students answer questions covered in previous sections of the textbook as preparation for the chapter content. **(GENERAL)**

_ **Reading Activity,** SE. Before reading the chapter, students write down the chapter and section titles and what they think they will learn from each section. **(GENERAL)**

_ **Using the Figure,** TE. Students answer questions about the chapter opener photograph. **(GENERAL)**

_ **Identifying Misconceptions**, TE. Dispel the misconception that the class Reptilia is not successful. Students may believe this because of the extinction of dinosaurs.

Block 2

FOCUS *(5 minutes)*

_ **Bellringer Transparency.** Use this transparency as students enter the classroom and find their seats. **(GENERAL)**

MOTIVATE *(10 minutes)*

_ **Activity**, Favorite Reptile, TE. Have each student sketch a picture of his or her favorite reptile. Have volunteers share their drawings with the class and tell why they chose that particular reptile.

TEACH *(30 minutes)*

_ **Teaching Transparency, Section Outline.** Use this transparency to give students a framework for the information in this section. **(GENERAL)**

_ **Teaching Transparency, Key Features of Reptiles.** Use this transparency to summarize the key features of reptiles. **(GENERAL)**

_ **Teaching Transparency, Changes in Lizard Body Temperature.** Use this transparency to discuss how a lizard can maintain a relatively constant body temperature throughout the day by moving between sunlight and shade. **(GENERAL)**

_ **Data Lab,** Identifying Ectotherms, SE. Students analyze a graph to determine which animal species is most likely an ectotherm. **(GENERAL)**

_ **Datasheets for In-Text Labs, Identifying Ectotherms, CRF.**

HOMEWORK

_ **Directed Reading Worksheet, The Reptilian Body, CRF.** Students complete the exercises in this worksheet to help them understand the material as they read the section. (**BASIC**)

_ **Active Reading Worksheet, The Reptilian Body, CRF.** Students read a passage related to the section topic and answer questions. (**GENERAL**)

Block 3

TEACH (*35 minutes*)

_ **Quick Lab,** Modeling Watertight Skin, SE. Students use   grapes to model and compare water loss in different types of skin. (**GENERAL**)

_ **Datasheets for In-Text Labs, Modeling Watertight Skin, CRF.**

_ **Activity,** Comparing Eggs, TE. Students research the eggs of birds, reptiles, and amphibians and distill their findings into life-size, full-color drawings of different kinds of eggs. (**ADVANCED**)

_ **Teaching Transparency, Reptilian Heart Structure.** Use this transparency to discuss the structure of the reptilian heart. Point out that in most reptiles the septum extends into the ventricle. (**GENERAL**)

_ **Teaching Tip,** Surface Area, TE. Ask students which melts faster,cubes of ice or a block of ice of the same weight. Lead students in a discussion of the importance of surface area in living things. Relate the cubes of ice to alveoli in   the lungs. (**BASIC**)

CLOSE (*10 minutes*)

_ **Reteaching,** TE. Have students pair up and list each of the seven key features of reptiles on individual index cards. On the back of each card, have students write a one-word clue to identify the characteristic on the front of the card. (**BASIC**)

HOMEWORK

_ **Quiz,** TE. Students answer questions that review the section material. (**GENERAL**)

_ **Section Review,** SE. Assign questions 1–6 for review, homework, or quiz. (**GENERAL**)

_ **Alternative Assessment**, TE. Have teams of students write brief descriptions of the five most important things they have learned about reptiles. (**GENERAL**)

_ **Quiz, CRF.** This quiz consists of ten multiple choice and matching questions that review the section's main concepts. (**BASIC**) **Also in Spanish.**

Other Resource Options

_ **Internet Connect.** Students can research Internet sources about Characteristics of Reptiles with SciLinks Code HX4038.

Lesson Plan *continued*

- **Internet Connect.** Students can research Internet sources about Amniotic Egg with SciLinks Code HX4005.

- **go.hrw.com.** For worksheets, videos, and other teaching aids related to this chapter, visit the HRW Web site and type in the keyword HX4 RPB.

- **CNN Science in the News, Video Segment 28 What's Slithering in Guam.** This video segment is accompanied by a **Critical Thinking Worksheet**.

- **CNN Student News.** Find the latest news, lesson plans, and activities related to important scientific events at **cnnstudentnews.com**.

Lesson Plan

Section: Today's Reptiles

Pacing

Regular Schedule: **with lab(s):** 3 days   **without lab(s):** 2 days

Block Schedule: **with lab(s):** 1 1/2 days   **without lab(s):** 1 day

Objectives

1. Compare the four living orders of reptiles.

2. Describe the timber rattlesnake's adaptations for locating and capturing prey.

3. Compare the parental care of crocodilians with that of other reptiles.

National Science Education Standards Covered

UNIFYING CONCEPTS AND PROCESSES

UCP1: Systems, order, and organization

UCP2: Evidence, models, and explanation

UCP5: Form and function

SCIENCE AS INQUIRY

SI1: Abilities necessary to do scientific inquiry

SI2: Understandings about scientific inquiry

LIFE SCIENCE: BIOLOGICAL EVOLUTION

LSEvol1: Species evolve over time.

LIFE SCIENCE: MATTER, ENERGY, AND ORGANIZATION IN LIVING SYSTEMS

LSMat4: The complexity and organization of organisms accommodates the need for obtaining, transforming, transporting, releasing, and eliminating the matter and energy used to sustain the organism.

LIFE SCIENCE: BEHAVIOR OF ORGANISMS

LSBeh2: Organisms have behavioral responses to internal changes and to external stimuli.

Lesson Plan *continued*

> **KEY**
> SE = Student Edition TE = Teacher Edition
> CRF = Chapter Resource File

Block 4

FOCUS *(5 minutes)*

_ **Bellringer Transparency.** Use this transparency as students enter the classroom and find their seats. (**GENERAL**)

MOTIVATE *(10 minutes)*

_ **Demonstration**, TE. Obtain a picture of a skink and cover its body so that only its head shows. Ask students how to tell a lizard from a snake. Then ask how you could determine if an animal is a snake or a legless lizard. Have students answer this question as they complete this section. (**GENERAL**)

TEACH *(30 minutes)*

_ **Teaching Transparency, Section Outline.** Use this transparency to give students a framework for the information in this section. (**GENERAL**)

_ **Directed Reading Worksheet, Today's Reptiles, CRF.** Students complete the exercises in this worksheet to help them understand the material as they read the section. (**BASIC**)

_ **Real Life**, SE. Students investigate the pros and cons of using geckos for pest control. (**GENERAL**)

_ **Teaching Tip**, Dangerous Snakes, TE. Ask students which venomous snake is the most dangerous in the world. Ask why a particular species is considered more dangerous than others. Point out that several factors determine how "dangerous" a snake is. (**BASIC**)

HOMEWORK

_ **Active Reading Worksheet, Today's Reptiles, CRF.** Students read a passage related to the section topic and answer questions. (**GENERAL**)

Block 5

TEACH *(30 minutes)*

_ **Up Close**, Timber Rattlesnake, TE. Use the teaching strategies and discussion questions in this TE item to guide students through this feature in the SE. Help students understand the rattlesnake's ability to sense its prey in the dark by using a warm object, such as a heating pad. Explain why it would be easier for a timber rattlesnake to kill a mouse than a lizard at night. (**GENERAL**)

_ **Teaching Transparency, External Structures of Snakes.** Use this transparency to discuss the rattlesnake's rattle and pit organ. **(GENERAL)**

_ **Teaching Transparency, Internal Structures of Snakes.** Use this transparency to discuss the venom glands, Jacobson's organs, reproductive structures, and spine. **(GENERAL)**

_ **Teaching Transparency, Orders of Living Reptiles.** Use this transparency to review the orders of living reptiles. **(GENERAL)**

_ **Teaching Transparency, Orders of Extinct Reptiles.** Use this transparency to to review the orders of extinct reptiles. **(GENERAL)**

CLOSE *(15 minutes)*

_ **Reteaching,** TE. Have students list characteristics of the four groups of reptiles. When the students have finished their work, have them share their results with a partner. **(BASIC)**

_ **Quiz,** TE. Students answer questions that review the section material. **(GENERAL)**

HOMEWORK

_ **Alternative Assessment**, TE. Students work in groups to research the reptiles of an assigned continent and make drawings. Display the drawings in the form of a mural of the continents. **(GENERAL)**

_ **Quiz, CRF.** This quiz consists of ten multiple choice and matching questions that review the section's main concepts. **(BASIC) Also in Spanish.**

_ **Section Review,** SE. Assign questions 1–6 for review, homework, or quiz. **(GENERAL)**

Optional Blocks

LAB *(45 minutes)*

_ **Exploration Lab, Using a Dichotomous Key to Identify Lizards, CRF.** Students use a dichotomous key to identify lizards. **(GENERAL)**

Other Resource Options

_ **Occupational Application Worksheet, Emergency Medical Technician, One-Stop Planner.** Students read about what an emergency medical technician does and fill out a worksheet on procedures and equipment used by emergency medical technicians. **(GENERAL)**

_ **Internet Connect.** Students can research Internet sources about Adaptations of Reptiles with SciLinks Code HX4003.

_ **go.hrw.com.** For worksheets, videos, and other teaching aids related to this chapter, visit the HRW Web site and type in the keyword HX4 RPB.

_ **CNN Student News.** Find the latest news, lesson plans, and activities related to important scientific events at **cnnstudentnews.com**.

Lesson Plan

Section: Characteristics and Diversity of Birds

Pacing

Regular Schedule: **with lab(s):** 4 days   **without lab(s):** 2 days

Block Schedule: **with lab(s):** 2 days   **without lab(s):** 1 day

Objectives

1. Summarize the key characteristics of birds.

2. Describe how a bird's feathers and bone structure aid flight.

3. Summarize how a bird's lungs and heart are adapted for high efficiency.

4. Relate the structure of a bird's feet and beak to its habits and diet.

National Science Education Standards Covered

UNIFYING CONCEPTS AND PROCESSES

UCP1: Systems, order, and organization

UCP2: Evidence, models, and explanation

UCP5: Form and function

SCIENCE AS INQUIRY

SI1: Abilities necessary to do scientific inquiry

SI2: Understandings about scientific inquiry

LIFE SCIENCE: BIOLOGICAL EVOLUTION

LSEvol1: Species evolve over time.

LIFE SCIENCE: MATTER, ENERGY, AND ORGANIZATION IN LIVING SYSTEMS

LSMat4: The complexity and organization of organisms accommodates the need for obtaining, transforming, transporting, releasing, and eliminating the matter and energy used to sustain the organism.

LIFE SCIENCE: BEHAVIOR OF ORGANISMS

LSBeh2: Organisms have behavioral responses to internal changes and to external stimuli.

KEY

SE = Student Edition   TE = Teacher Edition

CRF = Chapter Resource File

Block 6

FOCUS *(5 minutes)*

_ **Bellringer Transparency.** Use this transparency as students enter the classroom and find their seats. (**GENERAL**)

MOTIVATE *(10 minutes)*

_ **Demonstration**, TE. Bring a feather to class, and ask students what kind of animal it is from. Lead students to understand that having feathers is the key classification characteristic for the class Aves. (**BASIC**)

TEACH *(30 minutes)*

_ **Teaching Transparency, Section Outline.** Use this transparency to give students a framework for the information in this section. (**GENERAL**)

_ **Teaching Transparency, Characteristics of Birds.** Use this transparency to review the distinguishing features of birds. (**GENERAL**)

_ **Teaching Transparency, Contour Feather Structure.** Use   this transparency to illustrate how a feather keeps its shape and aids in flight. (**GENERAL**)

_ **Teaching Transparency, Avian Skeleton.** Use this transparency to discuss the main features of a bird's skeleton and how it aids in flight. (**GENERAL**)

_ **Teaching Tip**, White or Dark Meat?, TE. The color of dark meat in chicken is partly due to the presence of myoglobin, a hemoglobin-related molecule that helps provide oxygen to muscles that must contract vigorously and repeatedly. Ask students why duck breast meat and chicken leg meat is dark. (**GENERAL**)

_ **Teaching Transparency, Avian Heart Structure.** Use this transparency to describe the structure of a bird's heart. Point out that the ventricle of birds is completely divided by a septum. (**GENERAL**)

HOMEWORK

_ **Math Lab**, Calculating Average Bone Density, TE. Students determine the density of bone samples from two different animals. (**GENERAL**)

_ **Datasheets for In-Text Labs, Calculating Average Bone Density, CRF.**

_ **Directed Reading Worksheet, Characteristics and Diversity of Birds, CRF.** Students complete the exercises in this worksheet to help them understand the material as they read the section. (**BASIC**)

_ **Active Reading Worksheet, Characteristics and Diversity of Birds, CRF.** Students read a passage related to the section topic and answer questions. (**GENERAL**)

Block 7

TEACH *(35 minutes)*

_ **Teaching Transparency, Avian Lung Structure.** Use this transparency to discuss the evolution of lung structure. Inform students that birds have a high demand for oxygen. Have students trace the path that a volume of air follows through the respiratory system of a bird. (**GENERAL**)

_ **Up Close,** Bald Eagle, TE. Use the teaching strategies and discussion questions in this TE item to guide students through this feature in the SE. Discuss the size of bald eagle nests and the reduction in the numbers of bald eagles due to the use of DDT prior to its ban in 1972. Discuss their comeback and removal from the endangered species list in some states. (**GENERAL**)

_ **Teaching Transparency, External Structures of Birds.** Use this transparency to discuss feathers, grasping feet, eyes, and beaks. (**GENERAL**)

_ **Teaching Transparency, Internal Structures of Birds.** Use this transparency to discuss the brain, excretory system, cloaca, and digestive system of birds. (**GENERAL**)

_ **Teaching Transparency, Avian Adaptations.** Use this transparency to discuss how birds, their beaks, legs, and feet have been adapted to the particular environment they live in. (**GENERAL**)

_ **Teaching Transparency, Major Orders of Birds.** Use this transparency to describe some common orders of birds. Read the name of each order aloud so that students hear the correct pronunciation. Review the main characteristic of each order. (**GENERAL**)

CLOSE *(10 minutes)*

_ **Reteaching,** TE. Have students develop 10 questions based on the section content and usethem for a review game. (**BASIC**)

_ **Quiz,** TE. Students answer questions that review the section material. (**GENERAL**)

HOMEWORK

_ **Section Review,** SE. Assign questions 1–5 for review, homework, or quiz. (**GENERAL**)

_ **Alternative Assessment,** TE. Students work in groups to choose one bird adaptation and write a brief summary of the adaptation. Students should include a drawing with their summary. (**GENERAL**)

_ **Quiz, CRF.** This quiz consists of ten multiple choice and matching questions that review the section's main concepts. (**BASIC**) **Also in Spanish.**

_ **Science Skills Worksheet, CRF.** Students analyze information in a table about the four living orders of reptiles and birds. (**GENERAL**)

_ **Modified Worksheet, One-Stop Planner.** This worksheet has been specially modified to reach struggling students. (**BASIC**)

_ **Critical Thinking Worksheet, CRF.** Students answer analogy-based questions that review the section's main concepts and vocabulary. (**ADVANCED**)

Optional Blocks

LAB *(90 minutes)*

_ **Skills Practice Lab, Conducting a Bird Survey, CRF.** Students study six species of birds that live in the local area. They observe a variety of characteristics of the birds and use those characteristics to identify each species. (**GENERAL**)

Other Resource Options

_ **Exploration Lab,** Observing Color Change in Anoles, SE. Students observe the ability of anoles to change color when they are placed on different background colors. They also determine how this ability might be an advantage to anoles. (**GENERAL**)

_ **Datasheets for In-Text Labs, Observing Color Change in Anoles, CRF.**

_ **Teaching Tip**, Reptiles and Birds, TE. Students create a graphic organizer to compare reptiles and birds. A sample graphic organizer is provided in the TE. (**GENERAL**)

_ **Career,** Veterinarian, TE. Have students investigate the training required to become a veterinarian and find out where vet schools are located in your region of the country. (**ADVANCED**)

_ **Internet Connect.** Students can research Internet sources about Characteristics of Birds with SciLinks Code HX4036.

_ **Supplemental Reading, Through a Window, One-Stop Planner.** Students read the book and answer questions. (**ADVANCED**)

_ **go.hrw.com.** For worksheets, videos, and other teaching aids related to this chapter, visit the HRW Web site and type in the keyword HX4 RPB.

_ **CNN Science in the News, Video Segment 26 For the Birds.** This video segment is accompanied by a **Critical Thinking Worksheet**.

_ **CNN Student News.** Find the latest news, lesson plans, and activities related to important scientific events at **cnnstudentnews.com**.

Lesson Plan

End-of-Chapter Review and Assessment

Pacing

Regular Schedule: 2 days

Block Schedule: 1 day

KEY
SE = Student Edition   **TE** = Teacher Edition
CRF = Chapter Resource File

Block 8
REVIEW (*45 minutes*)

_ **Study Zone,** SE. Use the Study Zone to review the Key Concepts and Key Terms of the chapter and prepare students for the Performance Zone questions. (**GENERAL**)

_ **Performance Zone,** SE. Assign questions to review the material for this chapter. Use the assignment guide to customize review for sections covered. (**GENERAL**)

_ **Teaching Transparency, Concept Mapping.** Use this transparency to review the concept map for this chapter. (**GENERAL**)

Block 9
ASSESSMENT (*45 minutes*)

_ **Chapter Test, Reptiles and Birds, CRF.** This test contains 20 multiple choice and matching questions keyed to the chapter's objectives. (**GENERAL**) **Also in Spanish.**

_ **Chapter Test, Reptiles and Birds, CRF.** This test contains 25 questions of various formats, each keyed to the chapter's objectives. (**ADVANCED**)

_ **Modified Chapter Test, One-Stop Planner.** This test has been specially modified to reach struggling students. (**BASIC**)

Other Resource Options

_ **Vocabulary Review Worksheet, CRF.** Use this worksheet to review the chapter vocabulary. (**GENERAL**) **Also in Spanish.**

_ **Test Prep Pretest, CRF.** Use this pretest to review the main content of the chapter. Each question is keyed to a section objective. (**GENERAL**) **Also in Spanish.**

_ **Test Item Listing for ExamView® Test Generator, CRF.** Use the Test Item Listing to identify questions to use in a customized homework, quiz, or test.

_ **ExamView® Test Generator, One-Stop Planner.** Create a customized homework, quiz, or test using the HRW Test Generator program.

Reptiles and Birds

TRUE/FALSE

1. ____ Reptiles are found in every habitat on Earth.
   Answer: False   Difficulty: I   Section: 1   Objective: 1

2. ____ Modern reptiles are classified by the number of membranes found in their eggs.
   Answer: False   Difficulty: I   Section: 1   Objective: 1

3. ____ Both reptiles and birds lay amniotic eggs.
   Answer: True   Difficulty: I   Section: 1   Objective: 1

4. ____ Many reptiles regulate their temperature by varying their behavior.
   Answer: True   Difficulty: I   Section: 1   Objective: 2

5. ____ Most reptiles have a rapid metabolism and are endothermic.
   Answer: False   Difficulty: I   Section: 1   Objective: 2

6. ____ Reptiles, body temperature is mostly determined by the temperature of their environment.
   Answer: True   Difficulty: I   Section: 1   Objective: 2

7. ____ Reptiles have dry, largely watertight skin and lay watertight eggs.
   Answer: True   Difficulty: I   Section: 1   Objective: 3

8. ____ Reptiles reproduce by external fertilization.
   Answer: False   Difficulty: I   Section: 1   Objective: 1

9. ____ Reptiles must return to water to reproduce.
   Answer: False   Difficulty: I   Section: 1   Objective: 3

10. ____ Ovoviviparous reptiles carry their eggs in their bodies until shortly before or after hatching.
    Answer: True   Difficulty: I   Section: 1   Objective: 1

11. ____ The majority of reptiles are oviparous.
    Answer: True   Difficulty: I   Section: 1   Objective: 1

12. ____ Modern reptiles include crocodiles and alligators, turtles, the tuatara, and snakes.
    Answer: True   Difficulty: I   Section: 2   Objective: 1

13. ____ Turtles generally live on land, while tortoises generally live in the water.
    Answer: False   Difficulty: I   Section: 2   Objective: 1

14. ____ A sense organ in the tail of the timber rattlesnake helps it locate and capture prey.
    Answer: False   Difficulty: I   Section: 2   Objective: 2

15. ____ The age of a timber rattlesnake can be accurately determined by counting the number of rings in its rattle.
    Answer: False   Difficulty: I   Section: 2   Objective: 2

16. ____ An organ located in the roof of the timber rattlesnake's mouth helps it track prey.
    Answer: True   Difficulty: I   Section: 2   Objective: 2

17. ____ Crocodilians care for their young after hatching.
    Answer: True   Difficulty: I   Section: 2   Objective: 3

18. ____ Because of their small size, most birds are exothermic.
    Answer: False   Difficulty: I   Section: 3   Objective: 1

19. ____ Birds do not have teeth.
    Answer: True   Difficulty: I   Section: 3   Objective: 1

20. ____ Some feathers are specialized for flight.
    Answer: True   Difficulty: I   Section: 3   Objective: 2

21. ____ Down feathers cover the body of adult birds.
    Answer: False   Difficulty: I   Section: 3   Objective: 2

22. ____ A bird's skeleton is more rigid than the skeleton of a reptile.
    Answer: True   Difficulty: I   Section: 3   Objective: 2

23. ____ When birds fly, they use a considerable amount of energy.
    Answer: True   Difficulty: I   Section: 3   Objective: 3

24. ____ Birds meet their increased need for oxygen with lungs that have one-way air flow.
    Answer: True   Difficulty: I   Section: 3   Objective: 3

25. ____ Birds have a three-chambered heart.
    Answer: False   Difficulty: I   Section: 3   Objective: 3

26. ____ The way that air that passes through the lungs of birds is similar to the way that air passes through the lungs of reptiles.
    Answer: False   Difficulty: I   Section: 3   Objective: 3

27. ____ Oxygen-rich and oxygen-poor blood mix in the heart of birds.
    Answer: False   Difficulty: I   Section: 3   Objective: 3

28. ____ The shape of a bird's beak is a strong indicator of the bird's diet.
    Answer: True   Difficulty: I   Section: 3   Objective: 4

29. ____ The feet of birds are adaptations to specific types of environments.
    Answer: True   Difficulty: I   Section: 3   Objective: 4

MULTIPLE CHOICE

30. Reptiles are
    a. ectothermic.
    b. endothermic.
    c. ergothermic.
    d. None of the above
    Answer: A   Difficulty: I   Section: 1   Objective: 2

31. The skin of a reptile is
    a. moist and watertight.
    b. moist and thin.
    c. dry and nearly watertight.
    d. dry and permeable to water.
    Answer: C   Difficulty: I   Section: 1   Objective: 3

32. Reptiles respire through
    a. gills.
    b. lungs.
    c. their skin.
    d. spiracles.
    Answer: B   Difficulty: I   Section: 1   Objective: 1

33. Reptiles have
    a. internal fertilization.
    b. endothermic metabolism.
    c. a cartilaginous skeleton..
    d. All of the above.
    Answer: A   Difficulty: I   Section: 1   Objective: 1

34. Amphibian : moist ::
    a. ball : square
    b. oxygen : liquid
    c. reptile : scaly
    d. lung : primitive
    Answer: C   Difficulty: II   Section: 1   Objective: 3

35. The geographical range of reptiles is limited by
    a. length of day.
    b. moisture.
    c. temperature.
    d. topography.

    Answer: C   Difficulty: I   Section: 1   Objective: 2

36. Reptiles are least active when the weather is
    a. hot.
    b. warm.
    c. cool.
    d. very cold.

    Answer: D   Difficulty: I   Section: 1   Objective: 2

37. Which of the following is a reptilian adaptation to living on land?
    a. external fertilization
    b. endothermic temperature regulation
    c. respiration through gills
    d. the amniotic egg

    Answer: D   Difficulty: I   Section: 1   Objective: 3

38. External fertilization is *not* common on land because
    a. both sperm and eggs are at risk of drying out.
    b. sexual reproduction takes place more readily in rivers, lakes, and the ocean.
    c. most of the surface area of Earth is covered by water.
    d. All of the above

    Answer: A   Difficulty: I   Section: 1   Objective: 1

39. All reptiles except for crocodilians have a heart that has
    a. two atria and two ventricles.
    b. two atria and one partially divided ventricle.
    c. one atrium and two partially divided ventricles.
    d. two atria and two partially divided ventricles.

    Answer: B   Difficulty: II   Section: 1   Objective: 1

40. Which of the following is usually characteristic of reproduction in a terrestrial environment?
    a. external fertilization
    b. internal fertilization
    c. water-permeable eggs with no shells
    d. None of the above

    Answer: B   Difficulty: I   Section: 1   Objective: 3

41. During internal fertilization,
    a. a sperm is deposited directly inside an egg that is floating in a pond.
    b. males and females need not be present at the site of fertilization at the same time.
    c. a male deposits sperm directly into the female.
    d. a female deposits eggs into a nest, and the male covers them with sperm.

    Answer: C   Difficulty: I   Section: 1   Objective: 1

42. Some reptiles are oviparous. This means their young
    a. are nourished by a placenta.
    b. are born from eggs that hatch within the mother's body.
    c. hatch from eggs laid outside the mother's body.
    d. continue to develop in the mother's pouch.

    Answer: C   Difficulty: I   Section: 1   Objective: 1

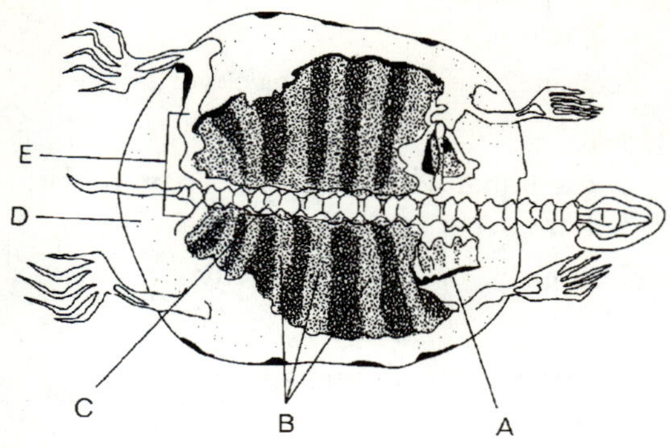

43. Refer to the illustration above. The vertebral column is labeled
   a. A.
   b. B.
   c. C.
   d. D.

   Answer: C   Difficulty: II   Section: 2   Objective: 1

44. Refer to the illustration above. The structure that has been removed is the
   a. skull.
   b. dorsal shell.
   c. carapace.
   d. plastron.

   Answer: D   Difficulty: II   Section: 2   Objective: 1

45. Unlike other reptiles, turtles and tortoises
   a. live only in water.
   b. are prehistoric.
   c. are endangered.
   d. do not have teeth.

   Answer: D   Difficulty: I   Section: 2   Objective: 1

46. Which of the following is true of snakes?
   a. They lack limbs.
   b. They lack movable eyelids.
   c. They lack external ears.
   d. All of the above

   Answer: D   Difficulty: I   Section: 2   Objective: 1

47. The tuatara is native to
   a. North and South America.
   b. Africa.
   c. New Zealand.
   d. every continent except Antarctica.

   Answer: C   Difficulty: II   Section: 2   Objective: 1

48. Snakes are reptiles of the order
   a. Squamata.
   b. Chelonia.
   c. Crocodilia.
   d. Rhynchocephalia.

   Answer: A   Difficulty: I   Section: 2   Objective: 1

49. The heat-sensing organs between each eye and nostril of a rattlesnake are the
   a. tracheal organs.
   b. Jacobson's organs.
   c. thermal organs.
   d. pit organs.

   Answer: D   Difficulty: I   Section: 2   Objective: 2

50. A rattlesnake can detect prey at night by using its
   a. rattle.
   b. eyes.
   c. pit organs.
   d. venom.

   Answer: C   Difficulty: I   Section: 2   Objective: 2

51. The fangs of a rattlesnake are used for
    a. reproduction.
    b. injecting venom.
    c. respiration.
    d. chewing.

    Answer: B   Difficulty: I   Section: 2   Objective: 2

52. rattlesnake pit organ : heat ::
    a. cat's whisker : light
    b. crocodile eye : heat
    c. earthquake seismograph : chemicals
    d. human ear : sound

    Answer: D   Difficulty: II   Section: 2   Objective: 2

53. Unlike other reptiles, crocodilians
    a. are viviparous.
    b. have a three-chambered heart.
    c. care for their young after hatching.
    d. reproduce by external fertilization.

    Answer: C   Difficulty: I   Section: 2   Objective: 3

54. Birds retain many reptilian features, including
    a. teeth.
    b. a long, bony tail.
    c. scales on their feet and legs.
    d. None of the above

    Answer: C   Difficulty: I   Section: 3   Objective: 1

55. A bird's crop
    a. temporarily stores food.
    b. is the first chamber of its stomach.
    c. is critical for flight.
    d. grinds and crushes food.

    Answer: A   Difficulty: I   Section: 3   Objective: 1

56. Birds excrete most of their nitrogenous wastes as
    a. urea.
    b. ammonia.
    c. uric acid.
    d. urine.

    Answer: C   Difficulty: I   Section: 3   Objective: 1

57. Birds are different from most reptiles in that birds
    a. are endothermic.
    b. have feathers.
    c. have four-chambered hearts.
    d. All of the above

    Answer: D   Difficulty: I   Section: 3   Objective: 1

58. Feathers are modified
    a. membranes.
    b. limbs.
    c. hairs.
    d. scales.

    Answer: D   Difficulty: I   Section: 3   Objective: 2

59. The bones of birds are
    a. composed primarily of keratin.
    b. solid.
    c. made of cartilage.
    d. thin and hollow.

    Answer: D   Difficulty: I   Section: 3   Objective: 2

60. A bird's skeleton
    a. is composed of thin, hollow bones.
    b. is more rigid than a reptile's.
    c. contains many fused bones.
    d. All of the above

    Answer: D   Difficulty: I   Section: 3   Objective: 2

61. The skeletons of birds are
    a. lightweight and rigid.
    b. lightweight and weak.
    c. solid and rigid.
    d. solid and strong.

    Answer: A   Difficulty: I   Section: 3   Objective: 2

62. Barbs appear on a bird's
    a. feet.
    b. beak.
    c. feathers.
    d. wings.

    Answer: C   Difficulty: I   Section: 3   Objective: 2

63. In birds, the power for flight comes from large
    a. wing muscles.
    b. breast muscles.
    c. shoulder muscles.
    d. back muscles.

    Answer: B   Difficulty: I   Section: 3   Objective: 2

64. A bird's heart has
    a. one chamber.
    b. two chambers.
    c. three chambers.
    d. four chambers.

    Answer: D   Difficulty: I   Section: 3   Objective: 3

65. Bird respiration is very efficient because
    a. bird lungs are small and hollow.
    b. only one lung functions at a time.
    c. the lungs have a special set of blood vessels.
    d. air flows in only one direction through the lungs.

    Answer: D   Difficulty: II   Section: 3   Objective: 3

66. The amount of oxygen a lung can absorb depends primarily on its
    a. thickness.
    b. position in the body of an animal.
    c. internal surface area.
    d. age.

    Answer: C   Difficulty: I   Section: 3   Objective: 3

67. The body temperature of a bird is approximately
    a. 41º C.
    b. 41º F.
    c. 37º C.
    d. 37º F.

    Answer: A   Difficulty: II   Section: 3   Objective: 1

68. The lungs of a bird are highly efficient because they are connected to
    a. gizzards.
    b. cloacas.
    c. air sacs.
    d. crops.

    Answer: C   Difficulty: I   Section: 3   Objective: 3

69. Talons would most likely be found among birds that
    a. eat seeds.
    b. grasp their prey.
    c. live in water.
    d. drink the nectar of flowers.

    Answer: B   Difficulty: I   Section: 3   Objective: 4

COMPLETION

70. Reptiles differ from amphibians in that reptiles have almost _________________ skin.

    Answer: watertight   Difficulty: I   Section: 1   Objective: 3

71. The _________________ egg is key to the success of reptiles as terrestrial animals.

    Answer: amniotic   Difficulty: II   Section: 1   Objective: 3

72. A reptile's body temperature is largely determined by the temperature of its
_______________________.
    Answer: environment Difficulty: I   Section: 1   Objective: 2

73. Reptilian limbs are positioned more directly _______________ their body than are
    the limbs of amphibians.
    Answer: under   Difficulty: I   Section: 1   Objective: 1

74. A reptile's body temperature is largely determined by the _______________ of its
    environment.
    Answer: temperature Difficulty: I   Section: 1   Objective: 2

75. Reptiles must remain _______________ during winter months in temperate
    climates.
    Answer: inactive   Difficulty: II   Section: 1   Objective: 2

76. The lungs of reptiles contain numerous internal _______________.
    Answer: folds   Difficulty: II   Section: 1   Objective: 1

77. Reptiles have dry, largely _______________ skin.
    Answer: watertight
    Difficulty: I   Section: 1   Objective: 3

78. Reptiles reproduce by using _______________ fertilization, which reduces the risk
    that gametes will dry out.
    Answer: internal   Difficulty: II   Section: 1   Objective: 3

79. The lower (ventral) portion of a tortoise's shell is called the _______________.
    Answer: plastron   Difficulty: II   Section: 2   Objective: 1

80. Turtles and tortoises lack _______________ but have jaws.
    Answer: teeth   Difficulty: II   Section: 2   Objective: 1

81. The _______________ is the dorsal part of a turtle's shell.
    Answer: carapace   Difficulty: II   Section: 2   Objective: 1

82. Unlike most other reptiles, _______________ are most active at low temperatures.
    Answer: tuataras   Difficulty: II   Section: 2   Objective: 1

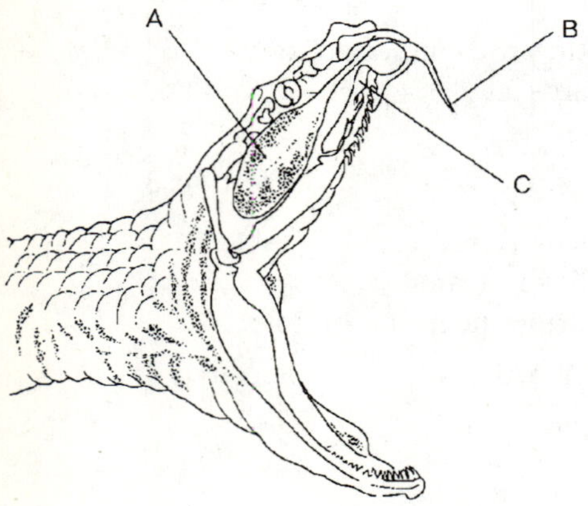

83. Refer to the illustration above. Structure C, which detects the odor of chemicals, is one
    pair of structures called _______________ _______________.
    Answer: Jacobson's organs
    Difficulty: II   Section: 2   Objective: 2

84. Refer to the illustration above. Structure B is a(n) _________________.
    Answer: fang   Difficulty: II   Section: 2   Objective: 2

85. Refer to the illustration above. Structure A is a(n) _________________ gland.
    Answer: venom   Difficulty: II   Section: 2   Objective: 2

86. Unlike other reptiles, _________________ care for their young after hatching.
    Answer: crocodilians Difficulty: II   Section: 2   Objective: 3

87. Feathers are modified reptilian _________________.
    Answer: scales   Difficulty: II   Section: 3   Objective: 1

88. Because of the way birds regulate their body temperature, birds have _________________ metabolism.
    Answer: endothermic Difficulty: I   Section: 3   Objective: 1

89. An adult bird's body is covered by _________________ feathers.
    Answer: contour   Difficulty: I   Section: 3   Objective: 2

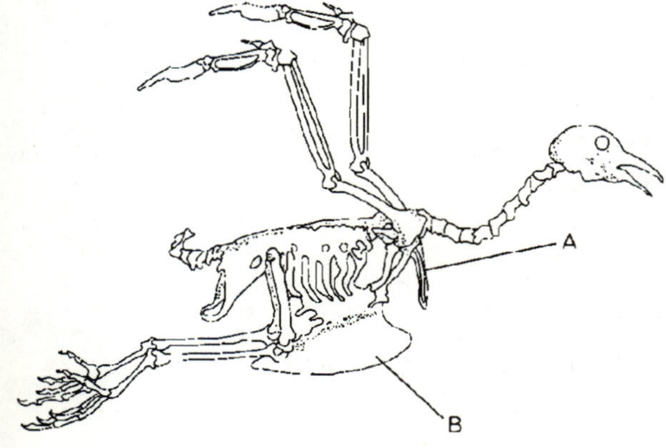

90. Refer to the illustration above. Structure B is the _________________.
    Answer: breastbone   Difficulty: II   Section: 3   Objective: 2

91. Refer to the illustration above. Structure A is the wishbone, which consists of the fused _________________.
    Answer: collarbones Difficulty: II   Section: 3   Objective: 2

92. The breastbone of birds is greatly enlarged and bears a prominent _________________ for muscle attachment.
    Answer: keel   Difficulty: II   Section: 3   Objective: 2

93. The fused _________________ of birds help absorb the stresses of flight.
    Answer: collarbones Difficulty: I   Section: 3   Objective: 2

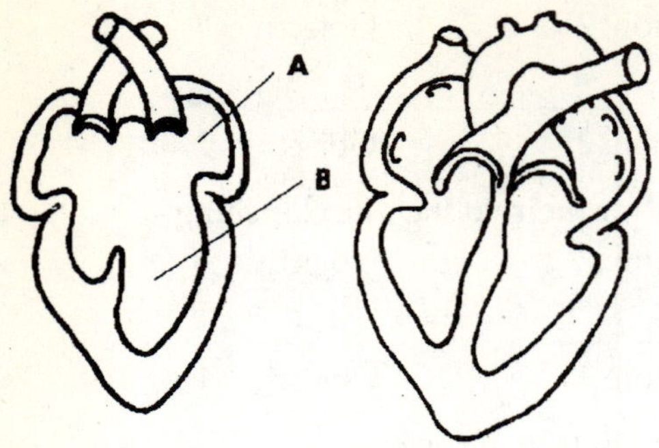

94. Refer to the illustration above. The diagram on the right is the heart of a
    ___________________.
    Answer: bird or mammal Difficulty: II   Section: 3   Objective: 3

95. Over the course of vertebrate evolution, a small amount of tissue from the
    ___________________ ___________________ has become the pacemaker in the hearts of
    birds and mammals.
    Answer: sinus venosus Difficulty: II   Section: 3   Objective: 3

96. The amount of oxygen delivered to body cells is increased in birds through
    ___________________ -way air flow in the lungs.
    Answer: one   Difficulty: I   Section: 3   Objective: 3

97. The avian heart has a completely divided ___________________.
    Answer: ventricle   Difficulty: II   Section: 3   Objective: 3

98. Birds of ___________________ have curved talons and curved, pointed beaks..
    Answer: prey   Difficulty: I   Section: 3   Objective: 4

99. The bills of ducks are ___________________ for shoveling through water and mud.
    Answer: flat   Difficulty: II   Section: 3   Objective: 4

ESSAY

100. Why isn't external fertilization an effective way to reproduce on land?
     Answer:
       Because external fertilization takes place outside the body of either parent, the eggs
       and sperm are at risk of drying out and dying.
     Difficulty: II   Section: 1   Objective: 3

101. As reptiles evolved, many were able to leave water and become completely terrestrial.
     Amphibians, however, are not totally free of water. Explain two reasons why these
     statements are true.
     Answer:
       Amphibians must remain near water because they depend on a thin, moist skin for
       oxygen and carbon dioxide exchange. They also need a watery environment to keep
       their eggs moist, and to enable sperm to swim to the eggs, which are fertilized
       externally. Reptiles, on the other hand, evolved lungs and a scaly skin that is almost
       watertight, making them fully terrestrial. Also, reptiles have internal fertilization and
       shelled eggs, so they can reproduce on land.
     Difficulty: III   Section: 1   Objective: 3

102. Support the statement "Crocodilians resemble birds more than they resemble other reptiles."

    Answer:
    Crocodilians are the only reptiles that, like birds, care for their young. They are also the only reptiles that have a four-chambered heart like that of birds.

    Difficulty: III   Section: 2   Objective: 3

103. How have the jaws of snakes and lizards contributed to the success of these reptiles as predators?

    Answer:
    The lower jaw of snakes and lizards is loosely connected to the skull. This loose connection allows the mouth to open wide enough to accommodate large prey.

    Difficulty: III   Section: 2   Objective: 1

104. Flying requires a great amount of energy. What adaptations in the respiratory system of birds allow them to meet their high energy needs?

    Answer:
    Birds have a system of air sacs that maintain a one-way flow of air through the lungs. In addition, air and blood flow in different directions in the lungs, increasing oxygen absorbtion.

    Difficulty: III   Section: 3   Objective: 3

105. The right and left sides of a bird's heart are completely separated, so oxygen-rich blood never mixes with oxygen-poor blood. Why is this complete separation necessary for birds?

    Answer:
    Birds need blood with a high oxygen content because flight requires large amounts of energy. The oxygen is used during cellular respiration to provide energy.

    Difficulty: III   Section: 3   Objective: 3